T0222355

IT DISASTER RESPONSE

LESSONS LEARNED IN THE FIELD

Greg D. Moore

Apress®

IT Disaster Response: Lessons Learned in the Field

Greg D. Moore
Brunswick, New York
USA

ISBN-13 (pbk): 978-1-4842-2183-9   ISBN-13 (electronic): 978-1-4842-2184-6
DOI 10.1007/978-1-4842-2184-6

Library of Congress Control Number: 2016961531

Managing Director: Welmoed Spahr
Acquisitions Editor: Susan McDermott
Developmental Editor: Laura Berendson
Technical Reviewer: Thomas Walsh
Editorial Board: Steve Anglin, Pramila Balan, Laura Berendson, Aaron Black,
    Louise Corrigan, Jonathan Gennick, Robert Hutchinson, Celestin Suresh John,
    Nikhil Karkal, James Markham, Susan McDermott, Matthew Moodie,
    Natalie Pao, Gwenan Spearing
Coordinating Editor: Rita Fernando
Copy Editor: Kim Burton-Weisman
Compositor: SPi Global
Indexer: SPi Global

Distributed to the book trade worldwide by Springer Science+Business Media New York, 233 Spring Street, 6th Floor, New York, NY 10013. Phone 1-800-SPRINGER, fax (201) 348-4505, e-mail orders-ny@springer-sbm.com, or visit www.springeronline.com. Apress Media, LLC is a California LLC and the sole member (owner) is Springer Science + Business Media Finance Inc (SSBM Finance Inc). SSBM Finance Inc is a Delaware corporation.

For information on translations, please e-mail rights@apress.com, or visit www.apress.com.

Apress and friends of ED books may be purchased in bulk for academic, corporate, or promotional use. eBook versions and licenses are also available for most titles. For more information, reference our Special Bulk Sales–eBook Licensing web page at www.apress.com/bulk-sales.

Any source code or other supplementary materials referenced by the author in this text is available to readers at www.apress.com. For detailed information about how to locate your book's source code, go to www.apress.com/source-code/.

Printed on acid-free paper

Apress Business: The Unbiased Source of Business Information

Apress business books provide essential information and practical advice, each written for practitioners by recognized experts. Busy managers and professionals in all areas of the business world—and at all levels of technical sophistication—look to our books for the actionable ideas and tools they need to solve problems, update and enhance their professional skills, make their work lives easier, and capitalize on opportunity.

Whatever the topic on the business spectrum—entrepreneurship, finance, sales, marketing, management, regulation, information technology, among others—Apress has been praised for providing the objective information and unbiased advice you need to excel in your daily work life. Our authors have no axes to grind; they understand they have one job only—to deliver up-to-date, accurate information simply, concisely, and with deep insight that addresses the real needs of our readers.

It is increasingly hard to find information—whether in the news media, on the Internet, and now all too often in books—that is even-handed and has your best interests at heart. We therefore hope that you enjoy this book, which has been carefully crafted to meet our standards of quality and unbiased coverage.

We are always interested in your feedback or ideas for new titles. Perhaps you'd even like to write a book yourself. Whatever the case, reach out to us at editorial@apress.com and an editor will respond swiftly. Incidentally, at the back of this book, you will find a list of useful related titles. Please visit us at www.apress.com to sign up for newsletters and discounts on future purchases.

—*The Apress Business Team*

This book is dedicated to Duke Moore, my father, the strongest man I've ever known. He taught me integrity, standing up for what one believes in, and going the extra mile. He also taught me my first puns and gave me a love of reading and writing. He had always wanted to write the Great American Novel.

Dad, I never could get you into a cave, but I can get you into a book. I just wish you were around to read it. It's not the Great American Novel, but I think you'd like it anyway.

Contents

About the Author

Greg D. Moore has been both an independent consultant (Green Mountain Software and the founder of QuiCR, LLC) and a director and later VP of IT at several internet startups that had 24/7 requirements. In both roles, much of his focus has been as a DBA. However, he has experience with networking as well as recent experience with programming. His blend of hands-on technical skills combined with his management skills gives him a unique insight into disaster planning. He has helped clients through disasters, as well as helped develop and test disaster plans, and experienced a few of his own.

Greg is also an instructor with the National Cave Rescue Commission (NCRC) and the Northeast Coordinator for the NCRC. He has participated in a several cave rescues, across four states, and has helped train hundreds of cavers and emergency responders across the United States and Puerto Rico.

About the Technical Reviewer

Thomas Walsh started his career in Emergency Medical Services in 1986, which grew from a college emergency squad to the director of clinical services for a local emergency medical services agency. He has experience as a volunteer firefighter, EMT, and paramedic in a variety of urban and rural health care systems. Tom has spent many years as a helicopter flight medic, where he gained significant insight into the aviation safety culture and high-stakes environment of critical care medicine. Tom is passionate about the education of new providers, health care system management, aviation, and health care safety. A prolific educator and lecturer, he is always exploring and studying human performance during critical events with zero-fault tolerances and high levels of stress.

Tom holds a Bachelor's of Science in Health and Biology from Excelsior College, received his paramedic training from Sand Hills Community College in Pinehurst, NC, and is a Certified Medical Transport Executive. Currently, he resides in the Albany, NY, area with his wife, Christine, and his daughter Emily, working as a paramedic clinical educator. Tom is a member of the adjunct faculty at Hudson Valley Community College paramedic program. He has a keen interest in aviation, health care, EMS, information management, space flight, gardening, and many outdoor activities. Yes, Greg has dragged Tom into a cave to practice the rescue of an injured caver.

Acknowledgments

First I want to acknowledge the IT teams I have had the honor and pleasure of managing over the years. We made it through Y2K and many other incidents together.

Second, I want to thank my fellow NCRC instructors and coordinators. You literally wrote the book on cave rescue. I'm proud to be among your numbers. I've learned a lot from cave rescue and hopefully have been able to apply a few of the lessons learned to here.

I would like to thank Tom Walsh, who has been a great sounding board and editor. Without your input and corrections, this book wouldn't be what it is today.

Finally, I want to thank my wife, Randi, and my kids, Ian and Rebecca. You've been a great support and my world would be less fulfilling and less beautiful without you.

Introduction

I grew up in a former railroad station, across the street from a firehouse, and one of my favorite shows was *Emergency!*. These may seem like incongruent facts, but they actually helped shape me in a number of ways.

I would watch as the firefighters would race to fires and would often discuss with my classmates the most recent big fire in town. While I was too young to join the fire department and moved away before I could become officially involved, I always had a great deal of respect for what they did. I recall when they upgraded from an ambulance that was essentially an oversized station wagon to an actual van that today we would recognize as being closer to what we think of as an ambulance. Later they upgraded again to what would definitely today be recognized as an ambulance. I didn't fully understand the changes. It was only years later that I realized that the training and tools were evolving. Early ambulance drivers were often the guys (and back then, most were men) that could drive the patient to the hospital as quickly as possible. Many were actually morticians. This was because many ambulances were basically hearses. If you think about it, a coffin and a litter both slide in the same way.

There wasn't much more requirement than driving fast. Over time, the EMS community emerged with the earliest EMTs and paramedics. People that previously would have died before they could get to the hospital were receiving treatment in the field that only a decade before was not possible.

Much of this was mirrored in the TV show *Emergency!* It wasn't until decades later I realized how much of an impact *Emergency!* had on the industry. There are many EMTs and paramedics today that say they got into the field because of that show. But *Emergency!* was more than just a TV show. It was almost a documentary based on a very famous paper written in 1966—now called "The EMS White Paper." Its more formal name is "Accidental Death and Disability: The Neglected Disease of Modern Society."[1] This paper revolutionized how we think about emergency medicine.

The history of railroads doesn't necessarily have a single seminal event like that white paper. But it is often said that the rules of railroads are written in blood. This means that basically every rule is there as a result of someone dying and the rule being put into place to prevent future such deaths.

---

[1] https://www.ems.gov/pdf/1997-Reproduction-AccidentalDeathDissability.pdf

One example is what is known as blue flag/signal protection. Simply put when equipment is being worked on, or for passenger trains, cars or locomotives being added or removed, a blue flag or signal is placed in such a way to warn all other workers that movement of the train or car in question could cause a serious injury or death. There's an additional detail to this rule that is important. A blue flag/signal may be placed by a member of one of the repair crafts. The important part is that it may be removed *only* by the same person who placed it or a member of the same craft. (Here *craft* is perhaps best defined as people in the railroad with similar job functions or skills.)

This detail on who may remove it is important because in part it means people with the same skills and knowledge and the ones in the best position to know if it is safe to move the car or train are protecting each other. It also means that for example an engineer or conductor, or even in theory the CEO of the railroad, cannot remove the blue flag/signal protection. Just because they may be considered to have a higher job position, that position doesn't give them the authority. Keep this in mind later in the book as we discuss things like the Incident Command System and Crew Resource Management.

So what does all of this have to do with a book on IT disasters? Good question. While I grew to love computers at an early age, I also grew to love understanding how disasters unfold and how we respond to them. Just as the EMS field and railroads have matured over time and introduced new best practices, and if necessary, removed outdated practices, so has the IT field.

Over time, we've learned better ways to respond to disasters—and equally important, how not to respond.

As I grew up, I started to get more involved in various outdoor activities, including caving. In 1999, I took my first class on cave rescue and I became hooked. I also took lessons from that course, specifically ICS, and applied them to our Y2K response six months later.

This book then is a result of my watching EMS evolve, learning how railroads worked, cave rescue, and more, and applying the lessons learned to IT.

I've enjoyed writing it and I hope you enjoy reading it. And hopefully, you learn something from it.

A Different Approach

There are many books out there written for disaster planning in the IT world. Most focus on very specific ideas or concepts, such as developing a backup strategy for on-site and off-site storage of critical data. Some books talk about developing and writing a disaster response (DR) plan. This isn't exactly one of those books.

Although there are some examples in this book and hopefully some useful takeaways, this book is more designed to make you think about how to approach a disaster, not the specific steps to take during a disaster. I will avoid the obvious things like, "make sure you do backups" (though you should).

For the most part I'll be using "We" in this book because though it's sort of a one way forum, I sort of see this as a journey we're taking together.

This book draws upon a diverse set of ideas and experiences—not all immediately associated with DR in the IT workplace. However, hopefully by the time you get done reading you'll see the relevance. And hopefully you'll have had some fun and learned something. Yes, I did say *fun*, because if you're not enjoying your job, my advice right now is to start looking for a new job and find one you do enjoy. I can safely say, overall, I have fun at what I do and I'm having fun writing this book.

© Greg D. Moore 2016
G. D. Moore, *IT Disaster Response*, DOI 10.1007/978-1-4842-2184-6_1

My background is primarily in the IT space. I've worked with computers professionally for over 25 years. I've helped write DR plans, test them, and in a few cases, implement them. I've also had to deal with disasters where there was no formal DR plan and we had to go by the seat of our pants. Most of those were successful, some weren't.

When I'm not found behind a keyboard I can often be found either caving or teaching cave rescue techniques. I'm currently the database administrator for the National Cave Rescue Commission and the Northeast Regional Coordinator. I'm also an instructor. This background has given me some unique thoughts about DR plans and some cross-domain knowledge.

I'm also an avid reader that reads across a number of disciplines and enjoy reading about how we think and process. Check out my blog at https://greenmountainsoftware.wordpress.com.

All of this comes into play in my DR thoughts and my ideas in this book.

What Is a Disaster?

"But I know it when I see it."

—Justice Potter Stewart

Sure, you may know a disaster when you see it, but sometimes it helps to have a working definition. For the purpose of this book, I will be using the following definition:

> Disaster: An unplanned interruption in business that has an adverse impact on finances or other resources.

This is purposely a rather broad definition so let's discuss it a bit and be clear about what I mean.

Your facility is struck by a truck and catches fire. The server room is destroyed in the resulting explosion and fire-fighting effort. That's pretty clearly a disaster. I don't think anyone would really quibble over that.

Your server is running fine one day when the power supply dies and you can't reboot it. That example is perhaps not quite as dramatic, but still a disaster.

Your printer runs out of paper and displays the dreaded [PC LOAD LETTER] in the middle of a report. Yes, this is a disaster using the definition and I quite intentionally include it as such. Sure the impact may be small. It might take you five minutes to reload it and carry on. But that's five minutes of your time you weren't expecting to spend on that. Now what happens if that report is the one the CEO needs in order to present to the board meeting in 15 minutes and now it will be late?

The point is, not all disasters have to be huge. In point of fact, most are not. If you think about it, how many times have you received a call that your data center has burned down versus the number of times you've received a call that a printer isn't responding?

Not all disasters are huge, but some are far more common than others. Any approach to disasters must take that into account. Also, many of the concepts are the same across the board.

I start in Chapter 2 by discussing what a disaster response is and why we even bother having one. This may sound like an obvious exercise, but the truth is, I've encountered companies where the attitude is basically, "eh, we'll deal with it when it happens." Or, they go to the other extreme and have 30-page documents on how to respond to a paper jam. OK, that last one might be a bit of an exaggeration, but it's not far from the truth. I've seen companies operate at either extreme and that's far from ideal. In fact part of the impetus for this book was a client who was planning to purchase hardware for a disaster response solution, but really didn't have a written policy on what would trigger such a response. The hardware was great, but I felt like they were missing something important. This is similar to a company having an *automatic external defibrillator* (AED), but not training employees on when or how to use it. Fortunately, AEDs are easy to use and fairly foolproof. However, the American Red Cross and other organizations still encourage training in how to use them. So simply having the equipment or even a written plan isn't enough if you don't know how to use the equipment or when to implement the plan.

Next, I'll talk about a concept known as the Incident Command System (ICS). This is covered in more detail on Chapter 3, but simply put it is a management structure developed to respond to "incidents" or in our case, disasters. I will often use the term *incident* instead of *disaster* because the connation of a disaster is a huge problem, when really we want to talk about incidents of all sizes.

In Chapter 4, I talk about *crew resource management* (CRM) and its development, and how it has made being a passenger in an airplane much safer than it was and how you can apply similar concepts to your disaster response. I'll drive home the idea of "make sure someone is flying the airplane."

I discuss the role of checklists in Chapter 5: why to use them, when to use them, and when not to use them. Although a checklist is very useful tool, it is not a panacea.

I'll also touch upon the roles of management and IT, and the people you hire or that hired you. This is covered in Chapters 6 and 7. People are a huge part of your disaster response. People with the proper training can make a huge difference in a disaster. We'll touch upon how being flexible in your management structure, especially during a disaster response can be a key factor in a successful response. And hopefully you'll start to look at the individuals in your organization and start to look at their strengths and weaknesses. This may encourage you to hire differently or increase training.

Since I've mentioned that disasters come in all sizes, we'll talk about size: it matters. Chapter 8 covers the small stuff and Chapter 9 the big stuff. We will also discuss how we really want to prevent a small disaster from turning into a large disaster. Pretty much all large disasters start out small. If we can keep them that way, we can make our jobs a lot easier. Chapter 10 discusses when a DR plan is not enough. DR plans are not magical panaceas. Having one doesn't guarantee you'll go through a disaster unscathed or without incident. In fact, I can almost guarantee that the disaster that you do have will have significant differences from what you planned for. However, we'll talk about why a DR plan is still of value. We'll discuss the strengths and limitations of DR plans.

Actual testing is one area that I've found far too few companies invest in. I talk about why this is critical in Chapter 11, as well as the pitfalls of not doing it, or doing it incorrectly.

In Chapter 12, I talk about disaster mitigation and prevention. Here I'm going to make a point that I often see overlooked. Sometimes the answer to preventing a disaster is not to add more hardware or procedures, but rather to simplify things.

And sometimes you can see disasters that are coming up. This may sound like it contradicts my definition of a disaster, but it doesn't. You can expect a disaster, plan for it, and prevent it. You can also expect a disaster, do no planning, and fail to prevent it. Or you can even expect it, plan for it, and still have issues.

In the epilogue, I pull everything together and summarize the journey we've taken together. I also provide a list of suggested reading. This is far from an exhaustive list. I only highlight a number of the books I've read and in some cases referenced in this book. But trust me, there's a *lot* more out there. Some are very specific, such as text books on ICS. Some are books that I myself have yet to read, such as *The Challenger Launch Decision* by Diane Vaughan (University of Chicago Press, 1996); it is a book that has long been on my reading list, but until now, unread.

Each chapter has a similar format. I introduce the concept, and when possible, I give some background, history, and references. Then I show how I apply it to DR planning. Each chapter ends with an actual real-world scenario that either happened to me or that I am familiar with. Finally, I dissect the example and show how the concepts in that chapter, and possibly others, apply.

So let's begin.

Real-World Example: Cave Rescue

I mentioned my background in cave rescue. In August of 2013, I received a call one evening from the then Northeast Regional Coordinator of the National Cave Rescue Commission that a rescue was in progress in Weybridge, Vermont, and that I should prepare to head up. About two hours later, the go order was given and I was in my car to find a cave I had never been to in a part of Vermont where I had never been before. I made it to the right field in the middle of nowhere in the middle of the night.

I popped out of the car, introduced myself to the Logistics Section Chief (more in Chapter 3 on who that is) and asked, "What do you need?"

The response was basically, "Go into the cave and take it from there."

I entered the cave, quickly oriented myself to the situation, and figured out who was who. Fortunately, one of the people I ran into right away was Steve Hazelton, a local caver and the head of the local cave rescue team. He was able to bring me up to speed very quickly. The quick summary is that a caver was attempting to free climb (that is, without any ropes) a section of the cave, when he fell and injured himself. This had occurred late in the late afternoon of the prior day.[1] I arrived at about 2:00 AM.

I soon made my way down a rope to the patient. He was with a fellow cave rescue instructor that I knew, Scott Stepenuck. Scott briefed me on the patient and we quickly formed the plan for the first part of the evacuation. This involved placing the patient into a special litter and hauling him up about 80 feet to the top of the first drop. I would be climbing a rope next to the patient, keeping an eye on him, and making sure that the ride was as smooth as possible. Before we began up, however, I introduced myself and told him, "I'd like to lie and say this won't hurt a bit, but honestly, it will probably hurt like hell. I'll do all I can to get you up as quickly and safely and as pain free as possible, but I can't do it completely painlessly." He simply replied, "That's OK. I just want to get the heck out of here."

We got him to the top of the first drop and then up to the top of another small chamber. At this point, we were only maybe 40 feet from the entrance. However, the entrance was about 3 feet tall and 18 inches wide, and it had boulders along the bottom. The original plan to move the patient out over this failed.

To quote Eugene Kranz of *Apollo 13* fame, "Failure is not an option." We obviously had to get the patient out. We tried one or two other things that didn't work. I then spoke with one of the fellow rescuers, Peter Youngbaer,[2] who I knew and whose advice I trusted. He suggested an idea. Fortunately, I knew

---

[1] http://www.wcax.com/story/23076860/crews-work-14-hours-on-vt-cave-rescue
[2] https://rigvertical.wordpress.com/weybridge-cave-rescue/

at least one of the additional rescuers, Mark Dickey, who was still outside the cave. I called for him to come closer. I introduced him to Peter behind me, told Mark what the plan was and what I wanted them to do, and gave them 15 minutes to do it.

Fifteen minutes later, they had a line run along the ceiling, which we called a *trolley line*, and basically put some carbineers on the edge of the litter and hauled the patient out of there, floating him above the boulders on the floor.

The caver was then whisked to the ambulance and taken to the hospital, where he could receive the advanced medical treatment he needed.

Now that I've told the story, I want to provide an analysis of it.

Analysis

I want to point out that this example is written in the first person, so my role is a bit magnified. I want to make sure that it doesn't sound like I'm taking credit for the hard and equally important work that others performed. In actuality, it was a team of people. I don't know the exact number of people involved, but underground there were easily 20 to 30 people, plus all the fire/rescue people on the surface. I had shown up several hours into the rescue, so a lot of rigging and rock removal had been done long before I got there. This was important to the success of the rescue.

Another very important part of the rescue was the rescue pre-plan. This was a document already developed by Steve Hazelton and other local cavers to plan what would be required to rescue someone in the cave from below the large drop. One of the things they realized was that a patient in a litter wouldn't fit through the top of the drop. So they knew any rescue would require people to remove rock.

That said, I use this example to tie together all the topics that I am discussing in one example.

ICS was used above and below ground so that the incident could be properly managed. An example of that was my ability to show up, know whom to speak to, what procedures (including a medical check-in and check-out) to go through, and how to perform a smooth transfer of management inside the cave from Steve Hazelton to myself.

In the event of the final rigging, I was able to use lessons learned from CRM (basically, clear instructions/setting clear expectations) and get the two riggers talking to each other while I monitored their discussion. (This was also an example of properly used ICS, by the way.) In addition, my discussion with the patient comes from a similar space.

While not exactly a checklist, the first rescuers on the scene had a plan that they could operate from. This saved a lot of time and helped them manage resources successfully. And once it became clear the plan we had had to be modified, we were able to go "off the checklist" and adapt and improvise while still doing things safely and successfully.

It should be clear there were multiple layers of management involved. Steve, and then I, handled some of the key parts within the cave. For a while, Scott handled the patient management. Peter and Mark handled the final rigging. We all reported to the Operations Section Chief, who reported to the Incident Commander. But equally important, many of us had common training. We were familiar with each other and knew we could trust each other's skills. We also knew if one of us was asked to do something beyond our skill set, we would speak up before it became an issue.

Also very importantly, the responding fire department very quickly knew that they did not have the skills and people to handle an in-cave incident. So rather than waste energy and resources, they called in the experts. This is an important skill that we'll talk about more under "people."

The pre-plan had been developed from prior testing at the cave and we've done at least one practice rescue since then. By doing the original testing, a useful plan was developed.

In terms of planning for the expected, as a result of this, the fire department has since asked for and received more training. Because the top of the drop is now larger, it is expected that more people may attempt this cave. This means future rescues may be more likely. So we're planning for future events.

And finally, of course, the rescue wasn't over once the patient was out of the cave. We had to derig, remove all the equipment, account for all the people, do a debrief, and get all the people safely home.

Instead of an injured caver, this could have been a failed server at a data center that needed to be replaced. Do you have critical IT resources, such as web servers, or database servers, or the like? Do you have a plan if they fail? Do you know who you would call in the event of a failure? Do you know how you would respond? What if something else comes up that you weren't expecting?

So, with that out of the way, let's get started!

Why Disaster Response?

In some ways, if you're asking *Why disaster response?*, you're probably already in trouble. The simple answer is because *stuff happens* (some have a bit more vulgar expression, but let's keep this as PG-rated as we can). So rather than address the question directly in this chapter, I want to discuss what I think a good or bad disaster response is.

Disasters happen. And you need to be able to respond. For the rest of this book, unless noted otherwise, I will use *DR* to mean *disaster response*. Recovery suggests returning things to the way they were before the disaster. This may not always be possible. And sometimes it may not even be desirable. But we need to be able to respond to a disaster.

If you have no planned response and the disaster is large enough, your response may be to simply throw up your hands and give up. On the other hand, it is quite possible to have a response that improves upon the initial conditions. For example, in Chapter 1, I discussed a successful response to a trapped caver in Weybridge, VT. One part of the response actually came months later when actual training was scheduled for the local fire/EMS departments. This training increased their knowledge base and helped to ensure that future rescues will go even more smoothly. So in this instance, it was a fairly major disaster where the conditions were improved.

© Greg D. Moore 2016
G. D. Moore, *IT Disaster Response*, DOI 10.1007/978-1-4842-2184-6_2

"If you choose not to decide, you still have made a choice."

—Rush "Freewill"

Disaster Preparedness

For any disaster, you need a response. Even not doing anything is a form of response. Because we adopted a rather broad definition of disaster in Chapter 1, it's only appropriate that we have a broad range of responses.

In almost every case, if you choose to do nothing, your lack of response will permit the disaster to continue and the negative effects to continue. For example if the printer continues to blink [PC LOAD LETTER], documents simply won't be printed. This will eventually annoy people. If the printer in question is the payroll check printer, I'm sure that pretty soon you'll regret your choice not to respond.

However, there are cases where the lack of a response may have a very limited impact and may in fact be the best choice. For example, let's say that you have a daily summary report that gets run every day. It fails on Saturday but runs fine on Sunday and Monday. The person who reads the report doesn't care about the Saturday report. In this case, your lack of response may be the appropriate action. In fact, it may be the best action. If it has failed only once within a year, and the reason is fairly innocuous—perhaps someone tripped over the power cord that morning and then plugged it back in (a disaster and response of its own), then spending time responding is a waste of resources. I'm going to come back to this in a bit, however.

In general, though, you should be prepared to have a response to any disaster. It is important, however, to decide what the appropriate level of response is.

Again, let's use the example of a printer out of paper. A ten-page DR document that outlines a response is probably not the appropriate response. A simple policy is enough: *We store the paper here. Put it in the printer and press the Resume button.* In fact, it's simple enough that you probably don't even have to explain it, other than to let folks know where the paper is, if it's not obvious.

Factors to Consider

When thinking about DR, you have to gauge several factors:

- The size and impact of the disaster
- The cost of the response
- The cost of not responding
- The likelihood of the disaster

If the cost of the response is greater than the cost of the disaster, then your best response is no response. In the previous example, responding to a single report failing once is almost certainly a waste of time and money.

In addition, any response to a kicked power cable that has only happened once is probably not worth the time or money.

Don't make the mistake of assuming that a disaster is a singular occurrence. You need to look over a time frame. Often in the insurance industry, or in weather forecasting, you hear references to a "100-year storm" or a "500-year storm." The idea is that a storm this large will only occur once every 100 or 500 years. As a result, the response is scaled to that. For example, not building and insuring a house to survive a 100-year storm is cheaper than building and insuring one to survive a 10-year storm. The assumption is that you'd be better off investing that money and if/when the 100-year storm hits, using the savings in your insurance to rebuild.

So, you build your house to survive the expected rainstorms, but not the rare hurricane. And if a hurricane does hit, you plan for the larger disruption. On the other hand, if you're building the local firehouse, you might spend extra money to build it to survive the 100-year storm. The reason for this difference is because when the 100-year storm *does* hit, you can expect all the other infrastructure around you to fail. You may suddenly find yourself using your firehouse to house all the people whose houses didn't survive.

Focus on What's Important

Let's get back to that kicked cable. Is it your 100-year storm or your expected hurricane? And in this case, you're not looking at just one kicked cable, but all the cables in your data center. Perhaps it's the first time for that particular server, but when you start to look over your data center, you find that on average, this incident happens once a week. But you happen to have 53 servers, so for any particular server, it only happens less than once a year. Which metric do you care about? Wrong answer!

How do I know it was the wrong answer when I don't know what you answered? Because the truth is, there's not necessarily any right answer. If 52 of those servers are redundant web servers, and kicking their power cords loose is annoying but causes no downtime, then you might not care at all. Except for that remaining one server, which is a non-redundant back-end SQL server that all the web servers rely on. Now, once a year, that server might suddenly have a million-dollar power cable. (We'll also talk about cascading failures and linked failures.) Or that fifty-third server is your home office *Minecraft* server that no one really cares about. In that case, it doesn't really matter, does it?

The point I want to drive home is to think about which metrics are important and why. And which response is the appropriate one. In some cases, it may simply be easier to just say, "Eh, it happens. When it does, we'll plug it back in and move on". Or it may be, "When it does happen, it has the potential to take us down for 30 minutes, in the best case, as the database server recovers. Or in the worst case, it takes six hours if the database is corrupted and we need to restore from backups." In the latter case, you might want a written DR plan.

But is that enough? Probably not. What if you look into dual redundant power supplies for each server? (However, adding hardware can introduce other failure modes, which we'll discuss later on with twin-engine aircrafts.) What if it's simply a case of rerouting the power cables to plugs against the wall so that people can't trip over them? What if these solutions cost $100K in new wiring and power supplies?

In my personal experience, we had a server that was attached to an external set of disks. We started to find that any work done in that cage that involved going behind that particular set of racks would often mean a failure. And what was worse, inevitably we'd notice the failure about an hour after the person in the cage had left and was on the train back home. After three or four times of this happening, we tracked it down to a loose SCSI cable. But without keeping track of this metric, we might not have noticed.

Our solution was actually in two parts. The first was to tighten the screws on the cable. The second was to actually add a step to our cage visit procedure. Before the on-site person left the cage for good that day, they'd check back with the person in the network operations center (NOC) monitoring things and make sure that server was having no issues. Once confirmed it was OK, they could leave the data center. After a few months with no problems, we considered the root cause solved and dropped this last extra step.

There is no simple answer or one-size-fits-all response here. Unless you gave your answer a lot of thought, it was probably wrong.

Large vs. Small Disasters

There are several take-always that I want you to have in regards to small disasters:

- They can happen with a high frequency ([PC LOAD LETTER]) but do not have a huge impact and do not require too much thought.

- They can appear to be infrequent (single kicked cable) but actually be part of a larger pattern and require more thought.

- Even after some thought, the appropriate response may be to do nothing or very little.

- Conversely, you may find the problem is far bigger than you think it is and it requires a detailed response.

- The response may be a change in procedures rather than adding more hardware. This is often a much less expensive approach and it is easier to implement.

Large disasters are generally more obvious. They are the ones that C-level folks often worry about the most. The truth is, they happen very rarely, but when they do, the impact can be devastating and can cripple or even kill a company. I include in these the complete failure of a key database, a SAN failure, a facility burning down, and more. And, in fact, these are all examples of scenarios I've seen firsthand or heard secondhand. I will use them as examples throughout this book. I will state at the outset that disasters at this level should almost certainly have a detailed response plan and that C-level management should buy into it.

When I first got involved in the dot-com industry, there was a lot of talk about the "five nines" of uptime (i.e., being up 99.999% of the time). That meant the goal was to have a web site up and running with only 5.26 minutes of downtime a year. It was a lofty goal. I saw many people claim that it was their company's goal. I saw even fewer actually achieve it.

I'm not sure where the idea came from, but I suspect some Chief Information Officer (CIO) read it in the back of some inflight magazine, the word spread, and then it came down from on high: "Hey, we need the five nines of uptime!" However, in many cases, no thought was actually given to *why* this was a goal or the cost of it.

Take it from me, having only 5.26 minutes of downtime in a year is expensive and very hard to achieve. But sometimes, the question that no one stops to ask is *Was it worth it?*. Believe it or not, oftentimes the answer is no. If say a newspaper site is down for 15 minutes once a week for maintenance, is it really going to impact the bottom line? Probably not, as long as it is not at a critical time. But by permitting that 15 minutes of downtime, you might be able to cut your IT infrastructure costs dramatically. Let's take two scenarios and play them out.

Planned Downtime

Maintenance is necessary. Upgrades are often necessary. Let's take the simplest example of applying patches. Most machines can apply a patch and reboot in less than 15 minutes. So, let's assume that you don't want any downtime. Your setup is a typical one with a web front end or two and a database back end.

Now, you obviously have redundancy because you planned for this. But, you should still need a detailed plan for the switchover, testing it, and the like. If you can blindly accept a down server, though, you can greatly simplify the process and perhaps even reduce your required infrastructure.

Unplanned Downtime

This is the worst kind, of course. It seems like it always happens at the worst time. Again, though, if you're willing to accept some limitations and downtime, you can cut costs. For full redundancy, in the event of unplanned downtime, you need fully redundant data centers with automatic failover of routing and Domain Name System (DNS) and data redundancy. This can get very expensive. Simply keeping your databases in sync between the data centers can require expensive solutions. On the other hand, using something like SQL Server log shipping can mean using a less expensive version of SQL Server and requiring less effort to set up and maintain. However, it means accepting some downtime because you may have to ensure that the last logs are applied and everything is up to date.

This was in fact a solution that I applied to one customer. Their original plan was to have fully redundant data centers with a storage area network (SAN) solution that kept their database servers in sync. When it became obvious the cost of this was too high, we moved to a solution that relied on using log-shipping and they accepted a four-hour downtime. The cost dropped by more than 50% a year. That was a huge savings for them.

A handy metric here is *How much money will you lose?*. If you're going to lose a million dollars every minute of downtime, then spending a few million on redundancy to get the five nines of uptime might be worth it. If you're going to lose a few hundred dollars per minute, it might not be worth it. If it's your personal web page where you host pictures of your cute cats, then it's certainly not worth spending money for the five nines of uptime.

Real-World Example: Smokehouse Fire

Years ago, I had a client that made smoked meats. I helped set up their network. They used the computers to track shipments, orders, invoices, and so forth. It was a fairly typical accounting package for a business of their size. However, due to a particular problem, their server was being unreliable. It wasn't a huge problem, but it was an annoyance. Fortunately for them, a server crash didn't really hinder business. The meat got smoked regardless. And if the server was down for an hour, it was just a matter of waiting an hour later to get out an invoice.

We were in the process of determining a fix when my vacation schedule interfered. I'd be out of the country for a couple of weeks. It seemed like a bad time to leave them with a flakey server. The simple, low-cost solution was to take my home server and swap out the hard drive and loan it to them. This apparently worked great. There was only a single issue with the server the entire time I was out of the country. The uptime was great; they were happy.

I flew back to the United States and called my then girlfriend. She said, "I've got good news and bad news. Which do you want to hear first?"

I replied, "The good news."

"Well, the good news is your computer is OK."

"Umm, what's the bad news?"

"The smokehouse burned down," she replied.

Yeah, I guess my computer being safe was the good news.

Analysis

The ultimate good news was that the client was able to recover from the complete loss of their infrastructure. This is something many businesses never do. One key reason was because they were able to retrieve the server from the building before it was fully consumed in the fire. One of the owners had the presence of mind to tell the firefighter, "When you go in, at the end of the hallway, there's a computer. Simply rip it out and bring it out here." The owner was smart enough to realize that as long as they had the hard drive, the rest was replaceable—even if ripping it out the wall damaged the case. Because I was still out of the country, they took it to another vendor in town, who was able to put it into a new computer and boot it. Within 24 hours, they had a minimum network up and running and they were able to contact vendors and customers to tell them what was going on.

Now, there were two reasons that the owner said to grab the server. One, she knew it was the quickest and easiest way to get things back up and running. Second, she realized she had made an almost fatal mistake. Earlier that day, she had brought in the backup disks (this was back when all their backups could fit on floppies) into the office to recover some data. And in a rush to pick up her daughter from soccer, she had left them all in the office. So their backup procedure nearly failed them.

There are six lessons to take from this example:

- The clients didn't need and they couldn't afford a complete off-site DR solution. Without a smokehouse, the lack of a computer network was minor. The solution matched their budget and their needs, even when the ultimate disaster happened.

- The client had a backup system in place and was familiar with it. She had used it multiple times to restore data from minor mishaps (miskeying an account, etc.).

- Small disasters are far more common, yet the big ones can and will happen.

- Don't violate your procedures without good reason. The client realized that she should have taken the backups with her when she left. (More depth in backups would have helped here too).

- The human factor can be a huge factor when it comes to both the cause of a disaster and the response. Where possible, a DR should minimize the potential negative impact of the human factor and maximize the potential positive impact.[1]

- When all else fails, adopt the attitude of "Semper Gumby" ("Always Be Flexible") and focus on what's critical (maintaining the data itself, not necessarily the computer or even the building that it's in) and be flexible in achieving that end goal.

This client was able to rebuild their business. The lack of a building meant they could rebuild a more efficient and better facility. So in the long run, despite a disaster, they ended up in a better position—and with an even better network.

Exercise

Before going on to the next chapter of the book, I ask that you write down a list of potential disasters. This list should include minor disasters (using our definition from Chapter 1) that are relatively small but common, and major disasters, such as fires, weather events, and the like.

---

[1]I'd like to give an example how to one could potentially address the human factor in this particular case. This event occurred over 25 years ago. Back then the most obvious backup solution was a local tape backup or floppies. These days, a common solution is to use on-line backup solutions (i.e. one where backups are done over the Internet to an on-line provider). This means there are no physical tapes involved and it's impossible to leave tapes on-site by mistake. This eliminates a potential human factor.

Give each disaster a ranking of likelihood (you can use whatever scale you want: 1–10, 1–100, etc.). Rank the impact on your company and add any pertinent notes. Finally, include whether you currently have a planned disaster response.

You should end up something that looks like Table 2-1.

Table 2-1. Incident Impact Matrix

Possible Incident	Likelihood	Impact	Notes	Plan exists?
Development printer fails	Low	Low	Developers can print to another printer	See notes
Payroll printer fails	Low	High (depending on day)	Only critical on payday	No
File server disk fails	Medium-Low	Low	RAID keeps initial impact low	Yes, extra drives are on premises
File server power supply fails	Medium	Low	Redundant power supplies keep impact low	Yes, we have 4-hour hardware support
File server fails	Low	High	We have no extra hardware!	Yes, we have 4-hour hardware support
Backup tape fails	Medium	Low	It probably needs cleaning; we can suffer one day's failure	Yes, see "Backup Documentation.docx"
Power to building interrupted < 4 hours	High	Medium	Old building but critical systems on UPS	Failover automatic; nothing required
Power to building interrupted > 4 hours	Medium	High	Old building; we need to look at generator	No plan
Experience 100-year flooding	Very Low	Very High	We are above known 100-year flood line	No plan
Fire in facility	Low	Very High	We don't have a plan for this	No plan; we need one

As you go through the various chapters of this book, hopefully you'll find yourself referring to this table and adding more rows as you think of more potential disasters. You'll add columns for things, such as if you have or need a checklist, or who is part of your ICS team for the particular event. This table should also aid you in deciding where to spend your efforts.

For example, I might focus on the "fire in facility" incident first, but leave the 100-year flood incident for later because it's such a low likelihood (although, as recent weather events have shown, old flooding models and other weather-related events may no longer be useful.)

I said that I would try to avoid the obvious advice, like "perform backups," but I think that this exercise is one that will serve you well as you go through this book. Once you've done this exercise, you can move on to the next chapter. Or, if you want to keep reading without doing this exercise, that's fine too. I'm not checking up on you.

Introducing the Incident Command System

So far, we've sort of skirted around the edges of what a disaster is, why you need a response, and some ideas of what a proper response may or may not entail. Now I want to start to get into some specifics. This chapter will cover a specific concept known as the Incident Command System (ICS). In this chapter, I'll use the word *incident* more often than the word *disaster*.

ICS was developed, in part, to help manage some of the largest disasters the US routinely faces; namely forest fires in the western states. It was developed as a result of a major fire in California that caused the loss of 16 lives and the destruction of 700 structures.

© Greg D. Moore 2016
G. D. Moore, *IT Disaster Response*, DOI 10.1007/978-1-4842-2184-6_3

There are entire books on ICS and I won't attempt to replicate them here, but I want to give some idea of how the concepts can be applied to your own DR issues. Before any diagrams or definitions I want to start with my definition of ICS. You'll find many definitions, but mine is: *ICS defines certain specific roles and positions. This provides a common language, or in computer terms, protocol, for various people to interact and coordinate.*

A note to understand about the specific roles and positions is that ICS does not require a separate person to fulfill each position. A person is required to fill the position, but a single person can fill more than one position and in fact can fill all of them. This is quite common for smaller incidents.

A key point of ICS is that it is designed to expand and contract as needed during an incident.

Let's start with what the principal roles within ICS are and then apply them (see Figure 3-1).[1]

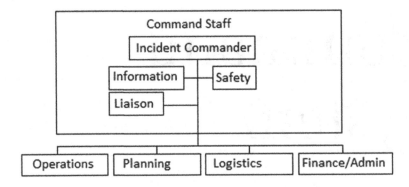

Figure 3-1. Basic ICS structure showing command and general staff

Command Staff

The Command Staff is responsible for the overall management. They control authority over an incident. This is accomplished by dividing the work into four roles: the Incident Command, the Public Information Officer, the Safety Officer and the Liaison Officer.

- *Incident Commander (IC):* Responsible for management and control authority over an incident, including setting incident objectives and ensuring that all responding entities meet these objectives

[1]http://ops.fhwa.dot.gov/eto_tim_pse/publications/timhandbook/chap3.htm, https://www.fema.gov/pdf/emergency/nims/NIMS_core.pdf

Note that this person can change during the course of an incident, especially if the size and scope of the incident expands greatly. For example, if it's a simple hard drive crash and no data is impacted, you might have the authority to swap out the hard drive and not have to involve anyone else. On the other hand, if the hard drive crash has taken down a critical database server, the director of Production Operations might be the Incident Commander (IC). If the incident is a breach of your data and a release of user IDs and passwords, the IC might be the Chief Information Officer (CIO) or even the Chief Information Officer (CEO).

- *Public information officer* (PIO): Interacts with the public and media and/or with other agencies with incident-related information requirements, and monitors public information

Generally, most IT incidents won't involve the public in the sense meant here. In most cases, these are the people within your organization. Think about the number of times that you've had to handle an outage and users kept popping into your office, or sending instant messages (IM), or calling you to ask, "Is the server up yet?" We all know it's often tempting to hunker down, fix the problem, and ignore all of these pleas for information, but they're important. Depending on the size and scope of the incident, you may want to appoint one of your team members specifically to handle all such questions—or you may want to even schedule "press briefings." If you're waiting for a tape to be pulled from Iron Mountain, shipped to your data center, and loaded, it may take hours. Not much will change during that time, but letting coworkers know every hour or so that things are still progressing as expected is better than no news. Contrary to the old saying, no news is *not* good news. It's simply no news and it lets folks use their imaginations to fill in the details.

However, for disasters that have a public-facing impact— say a web server outage, it may be critical to have a PIO that is providing information to customers, the media, and investors. This person must be authorized to make statements for the company (as any information provided may be used in future lawsuits, if they arise) and must be accurate and timely. While oftentimes the CEO may want to feel like they're taking charge by getting in front of the cameras, it is generally better if they work with a trained public affairs person to make sure that the information released is accurate and appropriate. A particularly apt example of bad information being released is the Sago Mine disaster in 2006. At 11:50 PM on January 3rd, news services started to report that 12 of the 13 miners had survived. The governor of West Virginia, Joe Manchin, proceeded to celebrate outside a church and told The Associated Press, among others, that there were 12 survivors. Unfortunately, he had not worked with his staff to actually confirm the rumors. The resulting confusion and emotional roller coaster made things much worse for the families of the miners.

Another example of poor public handling of a disaster was the Deepwater Horizon oil spill. Many credit former CEO Tony Hayward's comments as leading to his eventual resignation a few months after the initial incident.

In addition, the PIO should not assume that any particular method of communications will be available and should be well versed in multiple methods of sending out information. This may include the ability to set up conference calls for important customers, using Twitter, targeted SMS, and more. During our planning for Y2K, for example, we made the assumption that we could not use our web servers to relay information; so prior to Y2K, we built a list of critical customers to contact in the event that our site was down for an extended period of time and we arranged for multiple methods of contacting them.

- *Safety Officer (SO)*: Responsible to the IC for the set of systems and procedures necessary to ensure emergency responder safety, as well as the general safety of incident operations. The SO has emergency authority to stop and/or prevent unsafe acts during incident operations.

  You may think that you don't need a Safety Officer, but that's not always true. In a normal incident, you're probably right. So appoint yourself Safety Officer, look around, make sure there's nothing unsafe around you, and get to work. But consider what to do if the disaster is quite large. Perhaps the fire-prevention system in your data center has been triggered. How long before people can safely enter it?

What if your office is in the path of an impending blizzard and your CEO is urging you to send someone to the office on icy roads to ensure that the systems are shut down safely and all backups are brought off-site?

In the event of a larger incident where there may be a Joint or Unified Incident Command (e.g., the fire department responding to your data center fire has their own ICS) your Safety Officer should be prepared to brief his or her counterparts on any safety hazards they may not be aware of.

- *Liaison Officer:* The point of contact for representatives of other governmental agencies, nongovernmental organizations, and/or private entities.

    Again, at first pass, this may seem unnecessary, but if you cast it in terms of who to speak with when contacting a vendor, this makes more sense. Or perhaps you do need to talk to the fire department or other emergency services. If your building is on fire, you want to coordinate possible rescue and recovery operations with the fire department. In the smokehouse example from Chapter 2, the business owner and the fire department had to coordinate with the power company because the power lines were arcing against the aluminum side of the building. No one could enter the building to retrieve the server until the power was shut down.

General Staff

The General Staff is responsible for executing the actual response to the incident in question. This is accomplished by dividing the work into four roles: the Operations Section Chief, the Planning Section Chief, the Logistics Section Chief, and the Finance and Administration Section Chief (see Figure 3-2).

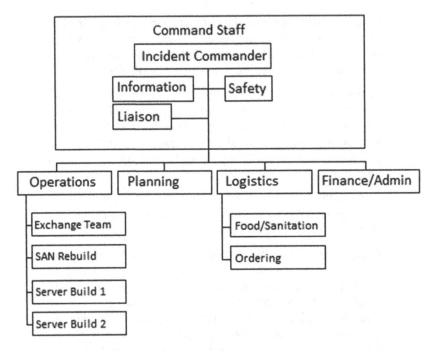

Figure 3-2. Expanded ICS structure

- *Operations Section Chief:* Responsible for all tactical operations. In IT terms, this is the person in charge of getting the next steps done. They may be replacing the hard drive or supervising the team rebuilding the disk array. They're the ones doing stuff or supervising those doing stuff.

- *Planning Section Chief:* Assists with the development of the *Incident Action Plan* (IAP), maintains resource use and situation status, and provides technical resources needed to particular aspects of incident response activities.

    This person is thinking ahead. After rebuilding the disk array, what else has to happen? Perhaps find the tape backups? Or if the data center was destroyed, they're planning what equipment needs to be acquired so that the operations section can start installing them. The Operations Section does the stuff that the Planning Section plans.

- *Logistics Section Chief:* This person acquires the required materials or personnel.

So while the Planning Section may say, "We need 40 servers and 10 switches here ASAP." The Logistics Section gets them. Or it may be, "We need a SAN expert on site in the next 24 hours. Find someone."

Sometimes, it's as simple as calling in the pizza order.

They're in charge of getting the supplies that the Planning Section needs so that the Operations Section can do things.

- *Finance and Administration Section Chief:* Tracks costs and accounts for reimbursements.

  While Planning may have great ideas and Logistics may be able to acquire the materials and personnel to execute them, someone has to approve it and pay for it.

  So Finance pays for the items and people Logistics is acquiring so the Operations folks can carry out the plans the Planning Section has developed.

The preceding represents the major components of an ICS structure. Within each section, there may be multiple teams and multiple personnel. In addition, the size and scope will almost certainly expand and contract over the course of an incident.

Keep in mind that these titles are actually functions, *not* positions. What this means is that someone has to do all of them, but each function does not have to be filled by a separate individual. This is part of the beauty of the ICS: it gives clear roles and responsibilities but it doesn't require a fixed number of people.

Small Example: CEO's Hard Drive Fails

Imagine the case of the CEO's hard drive failing in a typical IT shop. The IT person can single-handedly handle all the functions. They're the Incident Commander. They make decisions about how to solve the problem (swap out the hard drive). They're the PIO informing the public (i.e., the CEO) on what is happening, how long it should take, and which files may be casualties. In addition, they're also the Safety Officer. They're going to use a static strap to make sure that nothing gets fried. There's really no role for a Liaison here, but if there were, they'd be it also.

As for the General Staff, they're also fulfilling all the roles. The Planning Chief (i.e., themselves) decided that the plan is to acquire a new hard drive and to replace the failed one. The Logistics Chief (again themselves) knows the storeroom has an extra one and arranges for it to be acquired (i.e., walk over and get it out of the storeroom). Finance approves this because it's already a budgeted item. Finally, the Operations Chief gets it done.

One person has fulfilled all the roles and didn't even know it.

Medium Example: SAN Drive Failure

A slightly bigger incident may unfold as follows.

A sysops person receives an alert that the hard drive in the SAN has failed. Data is now at risk. At that moment, she's suddenly fulfilling all the roles in ICS. But she knows it's a bigger incident than she can handle.

She informs the IT Director, who decides that since this is the busy Christmas season, any failure beyond this could be a disaster, so they have to address the incident aggressively.

The IT Director begins appointing people (perhaps without them even knowing what ICS is) to fill roles. First, they take over most of the roles from the sysops person. She now becomes the Operations Section Chief. She's going to replace the drive when the time comes.

Meanwhile, the IT director calls the Chief Financial Officer (CFO) to tell her that he needs to get a spare hard drive drop-shipped, and although it is under warranty, there may be some additional costs. The CFO, realizing the seriousness of the situation, approves the purchase.

At this point, the IT director is the IC, Logistics, and Planning Section Chiefs. The CFO is now the Finance Section Chief.

Realizing that swapping a hard drive on the SAN has some risks (although in theory it's a routine operation), the IT Director calls his SAN expert and asks him to pull the "SAN Hard Drive Swap" procedure and review it to make sure that there's nothing else they need while they wait for the replacement hard drive to arrive. The SAN expert is now the Planning Section Chief.

Since Planning, Logistics, Operations, and Finance work closely together, and in return, report to the IC, they decide to all have a face-to-face meeting.

So sitting in an office now is the IT Director, the sysops person, the SAN expert, and the CFO. They are combining all the roles within ICS among four people. They have a quick 15-minute meeting to discuss any thoughts, issues, or concerns. The CFO suggests perhaps making another backup during the waiting period, "just in case." The SAN expert concedes that this is a good idea and, in fact, is part of the SAN hard drive swap procedure and is going to recommend it. The IT Director, who is the IC and the Logistics Section Chief, concurs and instructs an assistant to go get a spare tape.

After this, the IT Director, who is also the PIO at this point, drafts an email to key employees within the company, marked "Company confidential, not for public consumption." It explains what has happened, the planned course of action, how long it should take, the risks, and the steps being taken to mitigate them.

Four hours later, the new drive arrives and is replaced by the sysops person per the checklist provided by the SAN expert. The rebuild begins. Two hours later, all is safe again and the data is secure.

At this point, the IT Director tells everyone that everything is good and the CFO and SAN expert go home for the day. The IT Director asks the sysops person to write a quick after-incident report for review and tells her to handle things from there. At this point, the entire ICS has collapsed back to the sysops person, who completes the after-incident report, emails it to her boss, and then goes home herself. The incident is over and ICS (represented now by the sysops person) is disbanded.

Large Example: Data Center Fire

As a final example, let's imagine a major incident: a fire in the data center.

Again, this may start off very simply, with the first person on the scene assuming all the roles, but very quickly this is going to expand into a full blown incident command structure.

When your data center (or smokehouse) is up in flames, you'll need to really think about who is doing what. We're no longer talking about an incident that is contained in a few hours. We now have an incident that may take days or weeks to recover from (if at all).

Very briefly, you may have the following people in roles:

- *Incident Commander*: Chief operating officer (COO). With an incident of this scale, you need someone at the highest level who can authorize company-wide actions.

- *Safety Officer*: This may be someone familiar with the structure or other hazards. It might actually be someone working also as a liaison with the fire department.

- *PIO*: This is a person who can make authorized press releases to the public and to customers. Keep in mind that what this person says may impact how customers react. This person should be able to keep calm, cool, and collected while giving answers to questions. It should be someone who can answer questions truthfully while reassuring but not overpromising.

- *Liaison Officer*: This person will suddenly become hugely important. If your data center or office is on fire, they need to coordinate with the fire department and other resources to determine when it will be safe to re-enter the facility, if at all. If there are key physical items that are required, the liaison officer can coordinate with the fire department to remove them from the facility. Even if no one else has formal ICS training in your company, this person probably should have at least some training. In the case of a major incident, they should immediately find their counterpart in the IC staff run by the responding parties. They may also be required to work to set up what is known as a *Unified Command Structure*, but that's well beyond the scope of this chapter.

- *Operations Section Chief:* Probably your Chief Technology Officer (CTO) or the Director of IT. In general, I recommend that this be the person who has good hands-on experience and has a technical background. The person who does strategic, pie-in-the-sky planning for the company is not a good fit for this role. For an incident of magnitude, this person may be in charge of multiple teams such as a "network build team," a "VPN access team," a "server build team," and more. The scope and nature of these teams will change over the course of the incident. For example, there's no need for a VPN access team if there is no network to access. And in fact your network build team may simply become your VPN access team once they finish building a replacement network. Or at a certain point, say after a minimum of the network is functional, the operations section chief may think two members of the network access build team unnecessary and instead make them the nucleus of the VPN access team.

- *Planning Section Chief:* This person has to think in terms of short-term goals and long-term goals. The short term may include ensuring that all people are accounted for, and determining the hardware and services that are a total loss, what can be mitigated, and what has to be rebuilt from scratch. This person doesn't necessarily need operational experience (i.e., they don't need to know how to replace a hard drive). They do, however, need to understand how the company operates and be able to work with others to determine goals and the order in which to complete them.

- *Logistics Section Chief:* If your company is large enough to have a procurement department, the head of that is probably the person you want here. In any event, this person should have a complete list of vendors and know who to talk to at the vendors to get required equipment and how to reach them 24 hours a day. They should also be able to access people that may be needed. This could include employees, customers, and consultants. They may be tasked with ordering 20 servers one minute and then 3 hours later, with finding temporary office space for 100 employees, and then later be tasked with finding a network expert to help with the rebuild process.

- *Finance Section Chief:* This is probably the company CFO or Controller. This person should be able to write the big checks necessary and track all expenses, be it from ordering 20 servers to 20 pizzas for the operating teams.

In addition to the roles listed, you have to use another term that is part of ICS: *operational periods*. You can't have individuals working 24/7 for days on end. It won't work. And attempts to make it work not only fail, but inevitably make things worse. You have to determine how and when to be hand-offs. For example, your Finance Team may only need to be available from 9 to 5 after the first day or so. To get some sleep, your Operations Section Chief should be prepared to hand off ongoing operations to someone.

Another ICS term is *span of control*. A person should responsible for managing three to seven people at a time. If you find a team leader or a section chief managing more than seven people, it's time to break up the team into two teams. Each team should have its own team leader, who reports up the chain of command. If you find yourself with ten people on your server build team, you may want to consider breaking it into two teams. You can break this up simply as "Server Build Team 1" and "Server Build Team 2"—each with five members and with similar functions, but separate lists of servers to build. Or you may want to break it into the "Front-end Server Build Team" and the "Back-end Server Build Team." You may have 20 front-end servers, but they're all basically clones of each other, and only four back-end servers, but they each have unique requirements. As such, your front-end server build team might have three members and your back-end server build team has seven members. You might even break that into two teams, one as your "Database Server Build Team" with three members and the "Exchange Server Build Team" with four members. Later during the incident, you discover you need to rebuild your SAN so you work with Logistics and Planning to identify two more people and assign them, and one person from the Exchange Server build team (taking them from four to three members) to assist the new team. You have now formed a new, three-member team: "SAN Rebuild."

Meanwhile, your Logistics Section Chief has decided she needs to expand her teams. She creates a team to handle the ordering of food and to take care of sanitation needs. Also, due to the amount of hardware being ordered, she has decided to create a team specifically to handle the ordering and receiving of hardware. This is her Ordering Team.

From Figure 3-1, we've now expanded to a structure that looks more like Figure 3-2.

Once the various servers are built, the teams can then demobilize and get some rest or be reassigned to other tasks as necessary.

This means that Figure 3-2 will evolve over time as the incident evolves. Teams will appear as needed, merge into other teams, or be removed as appropriate. Eventually, Figure 3-2 will morph back into something closer to Figure 3-1, before it's finally dissolved.

Two items that should be clear from these examples is that anyone could be initially called upon to fill any role and that the person filling the role most likely will change over time. This means that during the initial phases of a disaster, it may be a very low level person who is your Incident Commander. Depending on the scale of the incident, this person may or may not be replaced. They might be replaced by another person because the scope of the incident has grown beyond their skills or the incident may last long enough that someone has to take over so the original staff members can get rest.

Another item that hopefully occurred to you is that an incident may quickly grow to the point where you need to interact with other agencies and that you may have more than one command system operating at once. For example, in the event of a building fire, you may be activating your own ICS to deal with your employees and data; meanwhile, the fire department has their own incident command system operating. But your system has to interact with their system. This is the concept of a Unified Command, which is beyond the scope of this book.

However, it may behoove you to contact your local fire department and other emergency response agencies before an incident to discuss the best way to operate with them.

In my role as the Northeast Coordinator of the NCRC, I have met with various local agencies and perform training with them, so that when an actual incident occurs, we are already familiar with each other's systems and know how to operate. This saves us a lot of confusion when an actual cave rescue occurs.

Real-World Example: Y2K

I'm going to break my own definition here just a bit and use Y2K as an example. Strictly speaking, Y2K itself wasn't—at least for us—a disaster (as defined in Chapter 1). It was a known event (programmers represented the four-digit year with only the final two digits, and the year 2000 was indistinguishable from 1900). However, since we couldn't test everything and there were a number of factors outside our control, such as the availability of power and communications, I decided to build an Incident Command staff and set up a war room for the evening.

Most people dread working on New Year's Eve, especially such a momentous one as that one, but in all honesty, that ended up being one of my more enjoyable New Year's Eves, largely due to planning. I should mention it helped that our war room was a large conference room in an old Federal-style brick mansion, complete with working fireplace! And yes, we did use the fireplace that evening. As part of the planning, we had our family members join us. This was for two reasons. First, it was more fun and easier to stomach working on Y2K eve as a group. Second, if there had been a large-scale power outage, we would all be in the same place. This would help relieve the anxiety of staff members who might have been distracted with worry about the safety of their family members.

At the start of the day on December 31st, we had a TV and several computers set up in our war room. Since we didn't expect any issues until much later in the day, I was the entire ICS Command Staff. At the time, I had two people reporting to me. One person was en route to our data center in New York City and the other en route to our data center in the northern Virginia area. I had spoken to the person headed to NYC that morning before he boarded the train. I had not spoken to the person heading to the other data center since the previous day, but I knew she was in the DC area and was doing some sightseeing during the daytime, so I wasn't worried.

As the day progressed, news reports about various Y2K issues came in, but none seemed worth worrying about.

At 10:00 PM, however, we started to build up the Command Staff. I had someone whose sole job was to be the PIO. They were to alert employees if there were complications and they had a plan for which customers to call and in what order, if something went wrong.

I had an Operations Section Chief now. He had taken over the monitoring and testing of the various parts of our infrastructure.

In addition to Incident Commander, I was still the Planning Section Chief since I had written all the response plans and had a good eye on the situation.

The CFO came in and became my Logistics Section Chief. Yes, the CFO was, in a sense, reporting to the Director of IT.

By about 10:30 PM, I was getting nervous. My on-the-ground person in NYC had made contact but my person on the ground in the Washington DC area had not. It was well past her check-in time. Since personnel are a Logistics problem, I asked the CFO, my Logistics Chief, to work on ways to find her.

She finally called in at about 10:45. Her cell phone had died and she couldn't find her charger. She was calling from a pay phone. Very quickly, the Logistics

Chief (a.k.a. CFO), the Planning Chief (me), and the Operations Chief put our heads together to form a plan. It was a gamble, but we counted on her being able to get into the data center and installing AIM on a server. We knew it was a risk since there were a number of ways that AIM could fail if Y2K was a problem (including losing power to the data center). In the meantime, the CFO, acting now as the Finance Section Chief, gave permission to buy another charger if she could find one in time.

During much of this time, we had the projector set up in the background. It wasn't showing critical information just yet. It was showing either *The Matrix* or *Enemy of the State*. I can't recall which one, but both are good movies.

At one point, someone brought in lots of food. We were set.

At 11:50 PM, I called a halt to the movie and we pulled up critical data on the projector. At 12:00 Midnight EST, we queried our servers, did some testing, and found absolutely no problems. By 12:10, we were descoping the team. The on-site people were released from duties, the Logistics and Finance roles devolved back to me. Operations and I discussed a few more things and by 12:30 AM EST, we called it a wild success.

We finished watching our movies and then went home to relax.

Analysis

This was a successful application of the ICS and shows how it expanded and contracted over the course of the incident. It also shows how your reporting lines may change over time due to the nature of the event. Had we had a major incident occur, the CEO, who was also there, would probably have taken over the function of the IC and started to call the shots.

This example is pretty anti-climactic. But that is the point. With proper planning and delineation of roles, a potential major event was strategized, an unexpected issue handled, and then the team dispersed. But had things gone badly, we would have been prepared.

The only incident of the evening was thinking that we lost someone, simply due to a dead cell phone battery.

Conclusion

ICS is used hundreds of times a day throughout the United States to handle everything from a single car accident to major forest fires covering multiple jurisdictions. ICS has a proven track record, and while there is a wealth of materials out there, entire courses that you can take, and jobs that are focused solely on ICS, a basic understanding of it can help you manage incidents at your company. You don't need to know every incident or even most of them. You'll probably never have to worry about having an Air Tactical Group Supervisor. But knowing the basic functions of the General Staff and the Command Staff is a great start. And again, think roles, not positions. In the case of the customer whose smokehouse burned down, almost all of these roles were fulfilled by one person in the first two to three hours. By the morning, some of the positions were devolved to other people, such as Logistics. But their entire company was about ten people, so they didn't need a huge Command Staff.

Another client of mine has more than 250 people at one location. Their DR plan is much more involved and fills most of these roles with separate people in the event of an incident like a fire or a major snowstorm that shuts down the offices for days at a time.

Recommended Resource

The US Department of Homeland Security's FEMA Emergency Management Institute (https://training.fema.gov/is/courseoverview.aspx?code=IS-100.b) offers an online resource for ICS 100-level training. I recommend that any person in your company that may be called upon to respond to any incident take and complete this training and get the certificate. It is estimated to take three hours to complete.

If after this you have personnel that want more advanced training, I suggest looking at what is out there and permitting them to take it. The more ICS skills that your staff has, the better prepared they are to react in an actual emergency.

Introducing CRM

"I'm in control here."

— Secretary of State Alexander Haig after the assassination
attempt on President Reagan

Like ICS, I'm going to give the most basic overview of what *crew resource management* (CRM) actually is. I'm going to blend it a bit with how NASA works mission control for space missions.

But let's start with a single, obvious rule: someone must always be flying the plane. This sounds obvious, but as you'll soon see, this doesn't always happen. A corollary to this rule is that only one person should be flying the plane.

Real-World Example: Eastern Airlines Flight 401 vs. US Airways Flight 1549

Rather than putting the example at the end of this chapter, I'll start with several examples and compare them.

On December 29, 1972, Eastern Airlines Flight 401 crashed into the Everglades near Miami International Airport. The only thing mechanically wrong with the plane was a burned-out indicator light that showed whether the front nose gear is down. There were 101 people killed on impact; there were 75 survivors.

G. D. Moore, *IT Disaster Response*, DOI 10.1007/978-1-4842-2184-6_4

On January 15, 2009, US Airways Flight 1549 made an emergency landing on the Hudson River. The airplane had lost thrust in both engines shortly after take-off due to multiple bird strikes. All 155 passengers and crew safely evacuated the plane and were rescued.

Why did one plane, with no serious mechanical defects, crash and kill over half the people on board, whereas another plane, with serious mechanical difficulties, execute a water ditching that resulted in no deaths?

Analysis

There are a number of factors that go into why, but one of the main reasons is that in the former case, no one was flying the plane—quite literally. The crash of Flight 401 (and other crashes) led to a focus of what was happening in the cockpit of these airplanes and how communications were handled.

There are multiple articles and books on these events, so I won't go into too much detail here, but I will give a brief overview.

Eastern Airlines Flight 401 had a three-person cockpit with a Pilot, First Officer, and Second Officer (Flight Engineer). Upon approach to Miami International Airport, when the crew attempted to deploy the nose landing gear, the indicator light did not turn on. This could have meant that the landing gear failed to deploy or that the light was burned out. The pilots attempted to cycle the landing gear and still failed to have the light come on.

They abandoned their approach and requested to enter a holding pattern so that they could work on the problem. Among other things, this included disassembling the light assembly and entering the avionics bay beneath the flight deck to observe the position of the landing gear via a porthole. This last procedure was complicated by the fact that it was nighttime.

During the event, the Pilot instructed the First Officer to place the aircraft in autopilot. Over the next three minutes, the plane lost several hundred feet of altitude. During the fourth minute, it lost another 250 feet of altitude— enough to trigger an altitude warning that apparently was not noticed by the crew. Within five minutes, the plane had descended from 2,000 feet to less than 1,000 feet and was still descending. Eventually, while executing a turn to bring the aircraft around, the Pilot noticed the plane was much lower than it should have been. Less than ten seconds later, the left wing clipped the Everglades wetlands and the plane crashed.

Apparently while the crew, along with a fourth employee who was deadheading (flying as a passenger while on duty) on the flight, were flying on autopilot, apparently the mode was changed from Altitude Hold to Control Wheel Steering mode in pitch. In this new mode, the autopilot maintained the last input for pitch on the aircraft; in this case, apparently a slight downward pitch.

During this time, all four people in the cockpit were focused on either the light assembly or the porthole in the avionics bay. Despite the warning chimes, no one noticed that the plane was losing altitude until it was too late. With four people in the cockpit, no one was doing the most critical job: flying the airplane. They incorrectly assumed that the autopilot was handling things.

Let's add another air crash into the discussion. United Airlines Flight 173 was on approach to Portland, Oregon, when there was an actual failure in the deployment of the right landing gear. The Pilot aborted the landing. At this point, the course of action was correct. The Pilot then proceeded to put the plane into a holding pattern while trying to diagnose the unusual failure.

The plane then proceeded to run out of fuel. It crashed six miles short of the runway. During this time, the other two members of the cockpit crew attempted to make the fuel situation apparent to the Pilot, but they did not succeed. Someone was flying the plane, but was not paying attention to a critical impending failure, despite warnings.

Flight accidents such as these were showing a general trend in human errors that were far worse than the original incident, compounding mechanical issues in ways that resulted in crashes.

The National Transportation Safety Board (NTSB) began calling for the development of what has become known as crew resource management (sometimes called *cockpit resource management*). There are several key components here that we'll discuss in a bit. But let's summarize by saying that it's important that there is a person who is actually focusing on the immediate problem at hand (keeping the plane in the air or keeping the site up and running) while the critical issue is being resolved and is open to input.

Let's move to US Airways Flight 1549, also known as the "Miracle on the Hudson." Unlike the previous incidents, which took place over several minutes and where the immediate problem was not life-threatening, the Flight 1549 incident took place over approximately 2.5 minutes and it was immediately life-threatening.

Approximately 30 seconds after take-off from La Guardia Airport, Flight 1549 suffered multiple bird strikes, which caused both engines to fail. This lack of thrust meant that the plane could not gain enough altitude to perform a standard go-around and return. Despite this, the plane made a successful ditching.

It's too long to re-create here, but if you read the transcript online, you'll see an excellent example of communications between the Pilot, the First Officer, and air traffic control (ATC). Solutions were offered and ruled out. Captain Sullenberger and First Officer Skiles communicated clearly. One item that you'll see in the transcript is a point when Captain Sullenberger clearly calls "my aircraft" and First Officer Skiles acknowledges it. This was a clear indication of who was flying the plane and that both members of the crew were aware of it. At other points, ATC and the First Officer offer suggestions, such as restarting the engines, or alternative runways or airports. Sullenberger acknowledges them and gives feedback on the usefulness of them. For example, he agrees with the engine restart procedure.

The lessons learned from a myriad of previous accidents came into play here and permitted a successful ditching.

Another example of the excellent use of CRM is United Airlines Flight 232, sometimes known as the Sioux City crash. This occurred July 19, 1989. While in flight, the tail-mounted engine suffered a catastrophic failure that resulted in the loss of all hydraulic systems. The hydraulic systems are necessary for the pilots to move the flight control surfaces. This failure essentially left the pilots with an aircraft that had functioning engines but the inability to turn, raise its altitude, or lower its altitude.

This was considered an unsurvivable situation. Despite that, with the efforts of the crew and a passenger who was a DC-10 instructor and offered his help, the plane attempted a landing. Although 111 people were killed, 185 survived.

Unlike Flight 1549, which was able to take advantage of existing checklists, such as restarting engines or preparing for a water landing, there was no established protocol for flying a commercial airliner without any hydraulic power.

Flight 232 began its flight with a three-person crew:

- Captain Alfred C. Hayes, 57, with over 7,000 flight hours in the cockpit of DC-10s.

- First Officer William R. Records, 48, with over 665 hours as a DC-10 first officer.

- Second Officer Dudley J. Dvorak, 51, with over 15,000 hours of total flying time; 33 in the DC-10 cockpit.

Not in the cockpit initially was training check airman Captain Dennis E. Fitch, 46. Hired by United Airlines in 1968, he had over 2,900 hours in the cockpit of the DC-10 and was assigned as a DC-10 training check airman at United's training center in Denver.[1]

At approximately one hour and seven minutes into the flight from Denver to Chicago, the fan disk on the tail-mounted engine broke apart. The resulting debris tore through the engine nacelle and sliced into a 10-inch wide conduit, through which the triply redundant hydraulic lines passed. The debris punctured all three hydraulic lines, allowing all the hydraulic fuel to drain out of the aircraft. Without hydraulics, and due to the other damage, the plane began a slow turn to the right.

---

[1]https://en.wikipedia.org/wiki/United_Airlines_Flight_232#Flight_crew

The pilots felt the engine come apart. Warning lights soon indicated that it was the #2 engine in the tail. Working under the premise that it was simply a failed engine, they began their standard checklists. It quickly became apparent that it was more than a simple engine failure when the plane did not respond to commands to control it.

Very quickly, it became clear that the damaged rudder was starting to roll and turn the plane to the right, with the nose pointing downward. Uncorrected, this would flip the plane and result in an unrecoverable dive into the ground. At this point, they set the left (#1) engine to idle and commanded full power on the right (#3) engine. This differential power recovered the aircraft from its immediate problem and began to level things out. This was not a perfect solution, however, as the plane entered a phugoid cycle.[2]

Captain Fitch was in the passenger compartment of the plane when he noticed the phugoid cycling. Knowing this was unusual and having heard the bang in the tail, he contacted a flight attendant, introduced himself, and offered his help. He was brought to the cockpit, where he introduced himself to the flight crew.

A mode that many airlines had previously operated under was that seniority mattered. Since many pilots come from the military, a strict hierarchy was the tradition and generally observed. While there are definitely benefits to this, it can also lock a team into a rigid pattern of decision making.

United Airlines had adopted CRM in the past few years and this was one of the first examples of its use in a critical incident. CRM has several important aspects but the following are among them:

- Introduction or opening: "Director of IT? I'm George. I'm from the SAN group". The point here is to make sure that the introduction or opening is to a specific person and they acknowledge your presence.

- Outline your concern: "The SAN has failing drives and I think the controller is bad because the failure rate is unusually high."

- Describe the problem: "At this rate, the SAN will go offline before we can get a replacement hard drive on-site and the SharePoint servers fail."

---

[2]Essentially the plane is climbing up and down. As it climbs, it loses airspeed, the nose pitches over, and the plane starts to descend. This causes the plane to speed up to the point where lift over the wing is increased and the nose pitches up and the plane begins to ascend. While generally not life-threatening, it can cause discomfort for passengers and experienced pilots are trained to detect and correct for it.

- Propose a solution: "I recommend we begin our DR plan to fail over to the backup SAN immediately."

- Get an agreement: "Do you agree? Can I begin?"

Note that the introduction, problem descriptions, and proposed solutions can come from anyone involved. The Captain of the plane, the Director of IT, or your Incident Commander still needs to make the final decision, but they're not doing so in a top-down authoritative manner. They're open to (and should actively be soliciting) input from anyone on the team.

In the case of Flight 232, the crew, with the addition of Fitch, were in completely unknown territory. The crew contacted the United Airlines maintenance base but was advised that, because it was considered virtually impossible to lose all hydraulics, there were no procedures or guidelines available. Flight 232 was literally flying into the unknown.

At this point, Fitch offered his help to the three-person crew. This meant there was another trained person who could provide help and input. Initially, he was asked to go back into the passenger area to see if the flight surfaces were responding at all to crew input. He confirmed that they were not.

He returned to the cockpit and again offered his help. At this point, the Captain was trying to fly the plane using the control stick and continuing to use differential power input to the engines. Upon Fitch's offer of help, Captain Hayes asked him to take over the throttles.

I'm not going to bore you with additional details of the flight, but I will highlight several salient points.

Despite a plane that was considered unflyable, the crew was able to divert to Sioux City Airport, where they attempted a landing. After discussion among the crew (again, a difference from a top-down authoritarian decision-making system), they attempted it with the gear down. There were several reasons for this, which the Captain agreed to.

Ultimately, the DC-10 attempted a landing at 240 knots, which was 100 knots over the preferred landing speed. Right before landing, the plane again entered a phugoid cycle and was unable to execute a flare, which required the use of the non-working flaps. This resulted in the right wing-tip contacting the ground. The plane broke up and the fuselage flipped over. Despite this, 185 (more than 62%) of the passengers and crew survived. Of the 111 fatalities, 17 deaths were due to smoke inhalation, not the crash itself.

This is a remarkable result considering that such an incident was not considered survivable and no one had experience in such a case.

There were several factors that came into play, but among them was CRM. In the words of Captain Hayes,

As for the crew, there was no training procedure for hydraulic failure. Complete hydraulic failure. We've all been through one failure or double failures, but never a complete hydraulic failure. But the preparation that paid off for the crew was something ... called Cockpit Resource Management... Up until 1980, we kind of worked on the concept that the captain was the authority on the aircraft. What he said, goes. And we lost a few airplanes because of that. Sometimes the captain isn't as smart as we thought he was. And we would listen to him, and do what he said, and we wouldn't know what he's talking about. And we had 103 years of flying experience there in the cockpit, trying to get that airplane on the ground, not one minute of which we had actually practiced, any one of us. So why would I know more about getting that airplane on the ground under those conditions than the other three. So if I hadn't used CRM, if we had not let everybody put their input in, it's a cinch we wouldn't have made it.[3]

I think that says it all.

Applying CRM to IT

In my experience, all too often the senior person comes in and starts to dictate the response. They know what's going on. They're in charge. That's why they have the fancy title in front of their name.

For what I'd call a "standard" incident, this may be appropriate. It may be as simple as pulling out the checklist and making sure that the steps are followed. If a hard drive fails, the checklist might suffice for solving the problem.

But let's consider an example where the CEO has to do a presentation before a large potential customer in the next 30 minutes and her laptop isn't connecting to the projector. This fits our definition because it is unexpected and it could impact the bottom line.

All the standard tricks aren't working, but the department secretary recalls that the DVI connector has been acting up and knows that the projector is a "smart" one and can support Bluetooth. IT never bothered to set this up and the CEO thinks Bluetooth can only be used to attach her earpiece to her cell phone.

---

[3]http://yarchive.net/air/airliners/dc10_sioux_city.html and Capt. Al Haynes (May 24, 1991). "The Crash of United Flight 232." *Retrieved 2013-06-04.* Presentation to NASA Dryden Flight Research Facility staff.

The department secretary decides that the IT person can solve the problem and walks over and introduces himself. "George. I'm Bob. I'm the department secretary. I was here when the projector was set up."

"Hey Bob. Pleased to meet you. We're in a pickle here. Got any ideas?"

"Sure. I remember seeing something about Bluetooth being enabled on the projector. Don't laptops have that? Could we set up the two using Bluetooth?"

"Hmm, you know, that just might work! Let's try that."

Five minutes later, the projector is working, the IT person is back at his desk, the department secretary is ordering lunch for the customers, and the CEO is doing her job. Incident managed.

Don't let seniority or experience get in the way of open communications. An important point to keep in mind is that it's not enough to say you have open communication; you have to actually practice it and encourage it, especially in an emergency.

While I started this chapter with an example, inverting the normal layout of my chapter format, I also want to end with an example. While I was an IT director at a company I worked for, I got a call one morning that a server was acting very slowly. This was causing performance issues. Rather than go into the office, I decided to start diagnosing it from home. Since the server was in a city 140 miles away, it didn't really matter if I was remotely accessing it from my house, or the office that was four miles away and only four miles closer to the server. I was working with my team and using a chat program to keep in touch with them.

Suddenly my connection to the server died and I was unable to ping the server. I hopped onto the chat program and asked the person in the office what had happened. "Oh, your boss came in and suggested we reboot the server. We figured he had seniority, so we did as he said." I slapped my forehead and cursed to myself. At that point, I figured I'd head into the office and deal with both the server and my boss there. The server issue was a bit more complex. It turned out we were tripping over a bug and had to work with Microsoft on a solution. This, of course, meant that rebooting the server didn't actually solve the problem; it just made it go away temporarily.

Fortunately, dealing with my boss was far easier. I basically told him that in the future, we both had to be very clear with each other and with the team who was in charge. While technically he had the authority to do what he did and he had he told me what he wanted to do, I would have acquiesced after making my argument for why it wasn't a good solution. I told him that we couldn't afford to have another case where the authority was split like that. Either he had to be 100% in charge or I had to be. It wasn't a matter of ego as much as a matter of making sure that we weren't confusing my team and that we weren't inadvertently making things worse. Fortunately, he saw my point of view and agreed. After that, we never had this particular problem come up again.

I revisit this topic of split authority briefly in Chapter 12, where I discuss Air France Flight 447, where it appears there was some confusion as to who was in charge of the plane and how CRM appears to have broken down as the events unraveled.

CRM has continued to prove useful over the years. It has been adopted by other industries because of its very real impact on safety and performance.

Checklists

What if I told you that a simple piece of paper could save lives in a hospital? What if I told you that in one hospital it was estimated that the use of this piece of paper saved eight lives a year and saved them nearly two million dollars?

You'd probably think that this was some sort of article on an advanced medical procedure or some sort of special training.

What if I told you it was a simple checklist? A nothing more/nothing less list. Basically, a list of things for a doctor to perform.

Up until that last part, you might think it pretty incredible—but then you might do a double take on the fact that a highly trained doctor, of all people, needs a checklist.

We probably all make lists. It might be a grocery list or a list of things to do today or this week. But shouldn't doctors know what they're doing and be beyond needing a checklist? Ironically, no. If anything, the more routine a procedure, if the risk is high, the more likely a checklist is needed.

In this particular case, the checklist was used to aid in the placement of central lines. This is a fairly routine and common procedure done thousands of times a day. But, because of the risk for infection, and in particular the type of infection, the risk is fairly high. In the original study of using a checklist on central lines, 11% of the patients became infected. Even if none of these resulted in deaths (and many do), this would be an issue because of the additional costs of a longer hospital stay, the use of antibiotics that may not have been needed, and other medical issues that could arise.

© Greg D. Moore 2016
G. D. Moore, *IT Disaster Response*, DOI 10.1007/978-1-4842-2184-6_5

This original study was done in 2001 at Johns Hopkins by critical-care specialist Peter Pronovost. It took some effort to actually get doctors to use a checklist, in part because it seemed beneath their dignity. After all, they were highly trained medical professionals, how would a simple checklist help them? Anyone with knowledge of medical history may recall the resistance that Ignaz Semmelweis encountered when trying to encourage his fellow doctors to wash their hands before delivering babies.

Fortunately, medicine has become a bit more fact- and evidence-based since then. But even then, there was resistance at Johns Hopkins and other locations where checklists have been rolled out.

But the results were dramatic: the infection rate dropped from 11% to practically zero.

However, checklists don't exist in a vacuum. In this case, Pronovost worked with upper management to ensure that nurses, who traditionally defer to the doctor's wishes and direction, were given the authority and backing to stop a doctor who was violating the checklist. (Note the aspects of CRM from the previous chapter, where input is encouraged from all ranks.)

I also mentioned that checklists are good for routine stuff. Perhaps a better choice of words would be for planned procedures. Surgeons, for example, still need to rely on their vast years of experience once they start cutting. They may use a checklist to confirm they're operating on the correct leg (yes, surgeons have been known to amputate the wrong leg at times). They may use a checklist to make sure their equipment is set up the way they want and that they've met the right anesthesia requirements, the right vitals, etc. But once they start cutting, they do have to be prepared for the unexpected. This is where their training comes into play.

For our purposes, there really are three types of checklists:

- Preventive/Before
- During
- After

You may already use some sort of change review planning before making changes to your infrastructure. This is essentially a checklist, even if you didn't think of it as such.

These types of checklists ensure that the system you are working on is in a known state. For example, before doing maintenance on a SAN to replace a drive, you might include steps such as the following:

1. Confirm that the most recent backup has been completed and is available.

2. Confirm that no additional drives have failed. If they have, you may need to revise your procedure.

3. Confirm that you have the right replacement drive in hand.

4. Confirm that you have identified the drive to be replaced.

5. Confirm that an anti-static bag is available for the failed drive.

6. Confirm that the required tools are in place.

If you can't confirm any of these steps, you need to stop and reevaluate.

During the drive change, you may want to include the following steps:

1. Ensure that no critical business operations are being done at that moment.

2. Perform the manufacturer's protocol for taking the failed drive completely off-line.

3. Turn screws below the drive to release the drive (note to self: screws above the drive belong to the drive above—do not release these!).

4. Once screws are completely unscrewed, pull the drive out. It should be removed with minimum effort. If it does not pull out easily, confirm correct screws have been released. If so, try again. If the issue remains, stop the procedure and evaluate possible causes.

5. Place the removed drive in the extra ESD bag.

6. Place the new drive into the now empty slot. Push until a click is heard and the face of drive is flush with others.

7. Confirm that the disk power light is on.

8. Tighten the screws below the drive.

9. Perform the manufacturer's protocol for bringing the new drive on-line.

Finally, after you've done all of this, you may want an after-action checklist that might include the following steps:

1. Confirm that RAID rebuild has completed.

2. Log failed drive serial number in failure database.

3. Fill out RMA information for failed drive.

4. Return the failed drive to the manufacturer.

5. Review the failure database to get a baseline of failure rate for drives in SAN. If it is not matching the manufacturer's MTBF, this may be cause for more investigation or cause to start purchase of a new SAN.

You're probably looking at all of this and thinking, "I already do that. I don't need a checklist." Let's just say, as the example at the end of the chapter shows, it only takes one mistake to show the value of having an actual checklist. Without one, you start to make assumptions, like the backup being good and complete. This will come back to bite you.

Further on in this chapter, I expand upon the ideas of these checklists.

Acronyms

In the meantime, I want to add in a very short form of a checklist: the acronym. Or more accurately, an initialization.

If you've ever taken a CPR or a first aid course, you probably remember being taught "Check the ABCs—Airway, Breathing, Circulation. That's your immediate checklist for what to do with an unconscious patient.

More advanced medical personnel may learn the term DOPE for when a patient who has been intubated is still desaturating (i.e., not getting enough oxygen.)

- Displaced breathing tube—check

- Obstructed breathing tube—check for occlusions or crimping

- Pneumothorax—check lung for collapse or change to the organ

- Equipment—check and assume mechanical failure, remove patient from vent, manual ventilations, is there O2 in the tank, etc.

This is designed to immediately take the patient out of harm's way and rapidly troubleshoot the issue. This may not solve every possible issue, but it gives the person providing medical care a place to start and solve the majority of issues without having to give it a great deal of thought.

It's especially important when developing this sort of "mini-checklist" that it be kept short and to the point, and that it cover the majority but not necessarily all possible scenarios.[1]

---

[1] Discussion of DOPE is thanks to Tom Walsh, paramedic and EMT instructor.

Checklists in Air Travel

Let's jump back a bit to commercial air travel. Commercial air travel has an enviable safety record, especially when compared to private air travel. A huge part of this is due to the use of checklists. If you've ever sat near the open cockpit door of a commercial aircraft, you've seen the pilots going over checklists. They may have flown that model plane 1,000 times and may have just landed at the airport to discharge and take on new passengers, but they will go through a preflight checklist. Well-trained pilots know that the checklist exists for a reason. It's when pilots get complacent and skip checklists that people can die.

How and when can you take advantage of this in your business? The answer—and most places know this and have already implemented it—are things such as change control plans and checklists for items such as server upgrades.

Checklists can be useful in preventing an incident and during an incident. Using the example of a central line, a checklist prevented the more critical issues of an infection. On the other hand, during a critical medical emergency, checklists are often used. Anyone who has taken a first aid or CPR course should recall being told to do things like to check the ABCs (Airway, Breathing, Circulation). This is a checklist—very short, but a checklist nonetheless.

Often, the process of creating the checklist can be as valuable as or even more valuable than the actual checklist. The reason for this is because to create an effective checklist, you have to question all the assumptions that go into it. Again, using the example of a checklist for putting in a central line, one step is to drape the patient to create a sterile area. No doctor would question this step and it's almost a certainty that all did so. But because it was left to their judgment as to what a large enough area to drape might be, there was no consistency in the procedure. Even if the doctors had at one point been taught the criteria, evidence showed that they often ended up not following their training. A formal checklist with the guidelines built in reinforced the criteria.

Also, during additional testing, it was found that a key piece of equipment was not part of the standard central line kit. This meant that its use was skipped at times. By soliciting feedback and working with the manufacturer of the central line kit, doctors would automatically incorporate this component.[2]

Ideally, checklists should be performed by two people. Having two people perform a checklist prevents cheating on the checklist. For example, if the checklists says to swab the area for 30 seconds, a doctor isn't tempted to swab for 20 seconds and say, "Good enough." The nurse can and should remind the doctor of the proper procedure.

---

[2]Atul Gawande, *The Checklist Manifesto* (New York: Metropolitan Books, 2009).

Having a second person also reduces the likelihood of a step being missed. If one person is doing the steps *and* checking them off, it's possible to be distracted or for your eyes to come back to the wrong line and to continue without realizing one missed a step.

Note that having two people perform a checklist is the norm in commercial aircraft operations. Two sets of eyes are better than one.

It's worth reiterating that when possible, especially for more critical operations such as commercial air travel or invasive medical procedures, that the second person have the authority to challenge, and if necessary, stop the procedure until the checklist is correctly completed. Keep in mind, it's not just a matter of saying that the person has the authority, but fostering an environment where people feel comfortable doing so and will do so. Part of this goes back to the lessons learned earlier from CRM.

Ground Control

An option that IT often has that airline pilots don't is the idea of "ground control." Shifting from commercial aviation, if we move to spaceflight, we see that we still (at least in the days of the space shuttle) have two people in the cockpit "flying" the spacecraft.

But as anyone who has ever watched the movie *Apollo 13*, or any other space movie, knows, ground control is always there—watching, observing, and giving input. One advantage ground control has is that it can see all the information at once and has instant access to dozens of experts who can provide information and feedback as needed.

In the IT world, we often call this the *network operations center* (NOC). I've always wanted to be an astronaut, so I think the term *ground control* is better. I'll use *ground control* even though I mean NOC.

Often times, the people in a data center are so focused on the tasks at hand that they may not be aware of a bigger issue or even an issue they caused. For example, someone is supposed to swap out the motherboard on a server but instead removes the wrong server from the rack because he failed to follow a proper checklist. Or, someone accidentally dislodges a cable to another server while removing the proper server.

Because they're so close to the problem and may not have a bank of monitors showing the status of the data center, they aren't aware of the new problem. The people in the data center should be in constant contact with their version of ground control as much as possible. And again, if it's just one person in the data center, often the person at ground control can be the other half of the checklist.

So you can imagine a conversation like this:

> Data center: "OK, I'm about to perform step 15: remove server USALB12DB05."
>
> Ground control: "Ayup, step 15. Go ahead and remove that server. The database has been shut down, so you're good to go."
>
> Data center: "Sounds good." [Starts to remove the server.]
>
> Data center: "OK, I've got the server removed. I'm about to open the case."
>
> Ground control: "Hold on a second. Can you check the secondary web server? I think it went offline when you removed the database server."
>
> Data center: "Sure thing." [Goes back checks the server, realizes it has a loose network cable, and plugs it back in.]
>
> Data center: "Yeah, the cable was loose. Apparently the tab on it is broken. I must have snagged it when I took out USALB12DB05. Let's make a point of replacing that cable in the near future so we don't have the problem again."
>
> Ground control: "Yeah, I confirm the web server is back up and running, so we're good on that. You can proceed to step 16 on the original checklist."

At this point, the person in the data center and the person in ground control continue to work on the original checklist. When they're done, they can then decide to either start a new procedure to replace the bad network cable, or if they feel the risk of something going wrong when doing so is too high (causing an unplanned five-minute outage on top of the accidental one they just had), they can postpone it for another time.

Planning for the Worst

Despite having a checklist, sometimes things go wrong. So what do you do? Have a checklist. In fact, I highly recommend that when you create a checklist, you have a two other sections: one detailing possible issues that could arise and the other the possible responses to the issues.

Now, at this point, most IT folks are shouting, "Duh, you're just describing a change control document!" Yes, I am. So if you already have this (and more), that's great. In fact, an actual change control document often has much more than what is in a checklist. But a checklist is a place to start.

Often when creating this part of the checklist, you'll think of issues that you might not have considered earlier. You realize that, if they do arise, you may not be prepared for them. I had a network engineer who was preparing a checklist and planning to do the work remotely. But when he started to do the risk analysis, he realized that his original plan had a couple of potential points of failure that, while remote, would have rendered the data center dead. He decided the best mitigation was to actually go on-site. That solved a slew of problems.

It should be noted too that sometimes the best response to an issue is to simply continue. I've had database upgrades where I realized that due to the scope of the data and schema changes, if a problem did arise at some point, it would be simpler, faster, and less dangerous to simply continue forward and work to solve the problem instead of trying to roll back. These are rare cases, but you need to know when they exist so that upper management can be warned and the side effects can be minimized. For example, if one of the database upgrades went wrong, our outage window would most likely jump from four hours to eight hours. But if we tried to roll back, the outage window would have easily exceeded eight hours. We felt confident that we knew which issues could arise and that they could be solved in less than eight hours, at the worst.

You may want to include a flow chart of potential issues and the paths to take when they occur.

I've also used a matrix in some change review plans (CRPs) to evaluate the overall risk. The following details some items for an example matrix, which is shown in Table 5-1.

- Estimate the complexity of the CRP on a scale of 1–4.

- Determine who might be impacted in a worst case failure and look in proper column for final "score."

- Scores from 1 to 3 require only an IT department head signature. (The department head may choose to require other signatures.)

- Scores from 4 to 6 impact the IT department head and the business department head. Additional signatures may be required as appropriate.

- A score that is 7 or higher requires CTO or CEO approval.

Table 5-1. Matrix to Evaluate Overall Risk

	Trivial	Fairly simple	Complex, or untested steps	Very Complex or Many untested steps
Impacts one service	1	2	3	4
Impacts department	3	5	6	7
Impacts entire company	5	7	8	9

Table-Topping

Another related concept to a checklist is the idea of table-topping.

In war movies, you often see the head military characters spread out a map on a large table and set up pieces that show the positions of their troops and the enemy troops, and play out the occurring or forthcoming battle so that they can see how things may end.

This type of procedure can be very useful for IT when planning a large operation. For example, if you're planning a data center move, I recommend investing in Visio software to create a set of templates for all of your equipment, including racks, and "building" a virtual copy of your current data center complete with racks and any other equipment that might be pre-installed.

Lay out each separate piece of equipment that you printed with Visio just as they are in your current data center. Then, as you move them, have someone take notes, essentially building the checklist as you go. You will quickly find any holes in your plan. "Oops, we can't move the load balancer until we have a working switch in the data center. OK, move the switch up to above the load balancer during the move." "Oh wait, we really don't need the backup database server until after we've moved everything else. Let's put that last on the list."

Once you have the process down and the checklist written to your satisfaction, repeat it. Get your team members to repeat it. It may be as simple as having them pick up the little piece of paper representing a particular piece of equipment from the table that represents your current data center and carry it to the table that represents your new data center and put it into its place on the printed "rack." This will get everyone familiar with their responsibilities during the actual data center move.

This obviously doesn't apply just to data center moves. It can be used for any large-scale operation. It could be used to verify a DR plan before actually performing a test, or worse, the actual DR plan itself.

This is also an excellent time to simulate a disaster. What if during the data center one of the trucks gets lost, delaying delivery? What if a server is dropped and damaged? Can you reconfigure the plan and still recover?

Now is the perfect time to practice.

In the cave-rescue world, we often do training in the very caves we expect to have a rescue in. This means packaging a healthy patient in the litter and trying to get them through the same obstacles that a real patient might face. If we can do it with a healthy patient, our chances of doing it with a real patient are much higher. On the other hand, if we discover we can't do it with a real patient, we know that we need to have a different plan for an actual cave rescue. (For example, due to prior practices, during the Weybridge Cave rescue we already knew how much rock needed to be removed to get a patient in the litter through the tightest spot.) This made the actual rescuer go faster and more smoothly.

Essentially, you're practicing in miniature before you perform the actual operation. The more practice, the less likely you are to have errors when you actually have to execute the operation. This is very much like airline pilots working in simulators for hours.

Not Using a Checklist

As valuable as checklists can be, they're not always the solution and sometimes they're not necessarily worth the time.

Commercial air travel uses checklists for everything because the cost of something going wrong is measured in tens, if not hundreds, of human lives and potentially millions of dollars in lawsuits.

I don't know a single driver, however, who uses a pre-printed, formalized checklist when they get in their car to go to the store for milk. There are several reasons for this. A car is far simpler to operate than an aircraft. Other than leaving the emergency brake on, there's little to keep a car from going when in gear and your foot is on the gas. Most drivers aren't going to do much more than check the gas gauge and make sure that the garage door is open before backing out of the car. A tire might be a little low on air, the windshield wiper fluid might be low, but the driver is going to be able to handle any issues between the home and the store. And if something does happen, we're not talking tens or hundreds of lives and millions of dollars in lawsuits. A formalized checklist for driving a car could easily take ten minutes. The drive to the store might only take five minutes. A formal checklist in that case is probably counterproductive and doesn't add much value.

Now imagine the same driver about to set off across The Rockies in the winter. Now they're probably going to have a checklist, even if it's informal, to make sure that the windshield wiper fluid is topped off, there's oil in the engine, and that there's warm clothing and maybe a bit of food in the back of the vehicle. The difference here is a higher risk of something going wrong.

Another case where a checklist often doesn't work is when entering the unknown. A surgeon may have a checklist going into surgery: make sure that it is the correct patient, make sure that it is the correct side of the body, make sure that everyone is sterile, and so forth. But at some point, you have to rely on the skill and knowledge of the surgeon, especially if complications are encountered that were not expected.

Real-World Example: Empty Database Copy

Back in 1999, when the Internet was still young, I was tasked with going to our data center and failing over the database server from the primary to the secondary one. This was to permit us to do some diagnostics on the primary one to determine why the floppy drive wasn't working properly. I didn't have a checklist, or as we later called it, a *change review plan* (CRP). (I ruled out calling it a Change/Review Analysis Plan for obvious reasons.) I was young, naïve, and a bit too confident. Besides, it would be a simple task; it was just a matter of clicking a few buttons to copy the database to the new database server and then updating a few web.config files so that the web servers would point to the new database server.

So, I pull up the dialog and begin the copy process. Nothing happened. Or rather, I didn't quite get the response that I expected. (I had, after all, tested this back in the office.)

I realized that I had a wrong setting and I needed to go back and change it.

And again, I hit the OK button and waited. It was done in no time. I was pleased and even a bit impressed at how fast things went. Then I realized it was too fast. I knew something wasn't right, so I started to poke around.

With growing horror, I realized that I had copied the *empty* database from the second server on top of the database on the first server. I can tell you from experience that copying an empty database is indeed fast. I now had two empty databases, one on each server, and no databases actually containing the data needed.

I wasn't too panicked at that point. Given the nature of our data, I realized that the backup from last night would contain almost all of our data and the data team could easily reload the data from that morning.

So I looked at the backups. There was no backup from the previous night. In fact, there was no backup for about a week. Now I was panicking. With a sinking heart, I called my boss to give him the bad news.

We weren't dead in the water, but this was clearly a terrible position to be in. So we quickly concocted a plan that I'd load the most recent backup that we did have and the data team would begin loading the last week of data. We'd simply accept being down for several hours. Besides the outage and the extra work on the weekend for our data team, this also meant that I would not be spending my afternoon trying to diagnosis the floppy drive problem. I ended up not being able to work on that problem until 2:00 AM the following morning. This was clearly less than ideal. After this event, I started to come up with the CRP that we used (with some revisions) over the next several years.

Analysis

A big point that I want to make with this example is where the value of the checklist would have come in. After hearing my story, some folks think that my checklist would emphasize clicking the correct button. They're wrong. The truth is, given the situation, I almost certainly still would have clicked the wrong button and caused the problem that I did. It was simply a matter of misreading, not misapplying the right steps. In other words, I did everything correctly—just on the wrong server.

While checklists are a great tool and can reduce the likelihood of mistakes or limit the fallout of a mistake, they can't necessarily eliminate all of them. For example, despite checklists, surgeons have still been known to amputate the wrong leg. In this case, a checklist would have assuredly told me to verify the server I was copying from and the server I was copying to. However, being human, I probably would have still made the same mistake.

No, the value in the checklist here would be the step to "ensure recent backup and perform one if there is none."

And this particular step would be the result of my reviewing all possible error modes. Now, I doubt "clicking wrong button" would have been on my list of possible error modes. However, "database becomes corrupt or unusable" most certainly would.

So, had I possessed a proper checklist in this scenario, I would have arrived at the data center, reviewed the backups, seen that there wasn't a recent backup, and immediately (possibly following another checklist or steps within the original) performed a backup. Then, when the problem came up, it would have been a matter of spending 30 minutes restoring the backup and being live again. And instead of an eight-hour outage that also required a remote data team to work on a Saturday, we'd have had a 30-minute outage and required no extra workers.

In fact, thinking about it further now, it dawns on me that if I had gone down the checklist route, I would have realized that I could have potentially used the backup to create the database on the second server and saved myself the risk of copying over an empty database. I believe I still would have gone the route I did simply because the permissions and other details were copied over by the GUI process.

Since that incident, I have always made a point of writing a CRP for any work I do. And I insist that anyone reporting to me have a CRP for any work that risks impacting the company's online presence. And then, I review the CRPs, or have someone review mine, for any holes.

Finally, if the potential risk is high enough when the actual work is performed, we revert to the ground control model and have someone remotely monitor everything and help confirm the checklist as work is completed.

The one time that I violated my own rules to a serious degree is an example for another chapter.

Roles of IT and Management

When people used to ask me my title, I'd say "Director of IT. That means if IT is broken, they call me."

It was a joke, of course, because I wasn't responsible for everything that was broken, but some days it sure seemed like it.

It may seem obvious that the role of IT is to keep Information Technology running, and the role of management is to manage. But what does that mean during an incident? As you saw in Chapter 3, ICS focuses on resolving critical incidents. It is a useful metric to start with in this chapter.

In this chapter, I'm going to break the discussion into the roles during a disaster or incident and the roles outside of that.

During a disaster, the roles may change because the immediate goal is solving the problem that caused the incident and restoring normal business operations. This means that the person who is best at making long-term strategic decisions may not be capable of making on-the-fly executive decisions that are necessary to restore order. Or, the person who is great at building servers can't see beyond that job and doesn't understand the business requirements necessary to restore order to the business.

© Greg D. Moore 2016
G. D. Moore, *IT Disaster Response*, DOI 10.1007/978-1-4842-2184-6_6

Before a disaster occurs, IT's role and management's role are much like what you read in typical books on the subjects. Management worries about the day-to-day and the future operations of the company, and IT helps provide the IT resources to carry out those operations.

In my experience, there's not enough conversation about disasters. For example, management may ask a question such as, "Do we have backups and extra equipment in case something bad happens?" IT's response is, "Of course." (At least that's the minimum it should be. If they don't have backups, they should!) But even though a question was clearly asked and answered, it's not enough. This sort of generic question is going to lead to problems if a major incident happens. Management should be asking very specific questions: "If the server supporting our payroll system fails completely, how long before we can print checks again and how much effort is involved?" "If our data center catches on fire, what's the plan?"

IT typically answers these questions in a specific manner. IT folks tend to think like a computer—in very specific and often binary ways. What needs to happen is a dialog. The responses should be more like, "Well, the payroll server is backed up nightly, and we have extra hardware to build something that should support it, but it may take a bit longer to process payroll. However, because of the proprietary nature of the software, we will most likely need to open a support ticket with the payroll software company to help things along. Can we assume someone will be available to authorize such an expense on short notice?"

"Oh, well, how much is a ticket?"

"It's $550 for a one-time ticket or $1,500 a year for four tickets. We average two to three tickets a year for other issues."

"OK. Let's get the four-ticket package. That way we're prepared and it's really not costing us anything more. Anything else we should be aware of?"

And thus the conversation continues.

As the Internet was becoming popular, the concept of "the five nines of uptime" became the goal for practically every site. By the strictest definition, which meant no downtime—planned or otherwise, a site or service was unavailable for less than 15 minutes a year. It's a noble goal. Companies bent over backward trying to reach the goal, but no one typically stopped to ask if it was a worthy goal. Management might say, "Of course it's a worthy goal! Our competition is doing it!" The IT response to that could be, "If our competition jumped off a bridge, would we?"

Sometimes management loses sight of what's practical and what's necessary. A bank, for example, might have a customer portal where customers can check their balance, sign up for services, and do other things. They may also have an online service against which credit card verification requests can be done.

The question should start with, "Do both sites require the same uptime?" The answer is probably not. The second site almost certainly needs a very high degree of availability. The former probably does not. If someone can't check their balance at 12:40 AM on a Saturday night, they're probably going to be OK waiting. At worst, they might write an email or make a phone call Monday morning, but they're unlikely to take their business elsewhere. However, if a credit card transaction can't go through, or worse, goes through multiple times, the customer is almost certainly going to use another bank's card, pay in cash, or even decide they won't buy that DVD at all. That directly impacts the bottom line.

So management and IT need to sit down and discuss what needs to be available, why, and the cost. It may turn out that the cost of keeping the consumer-facing web site available 99.999% of the time is so small as to not really matter, once other assumptions are made. In that case, the company is just as well off doing so. Or, both parties may realize that it will take what's essentially a fairly simple setup with some redundancy and turn it into a much more complex design that may end up costing five times as much as a design that is only 99.9% available. At that point, management needs to make a decision on what's important.

Hand in hand in this, both parties then need to have a discussion on priorities. A large-scale disaster may impact all of the company's services (such as a data center failure). There needs to be a discussion about which services are priorities, and why, and if there are mitigating factors that might change those priorities.

Using the same example, in the event that both services became unavailable, management would most likely want IT to focus on restoring the credit card processing service first and then the customer-facing page.

Once a disaster takes place, management's role often becomes subservient to IT's needs. Ideally, both parties have already agreed on the priorities of services to be restored and are aware of the expected time frames. For example, the company may identify the following items that need to be addressed during a major incident:

- External application programming interface (API) for processing of business with third-party vendors
- Consumer-facing web site
- Payroll
- Internal processing of orders and order fulfillment
- Manufacturing floor needs
- Email

- File services

- Internal SharePoint server

- External virtual private network (VPN)

- Internal network

- Internal Wi-Fi network

- Phone system

This is a lot for an IT staff to deal with during an emergency. And it should be obvious that it can't all happen at once. So, both sides have to sit down and prioritize. As an exercise, I suggest the following: IT creates its prioritized list and estimated times for return to service based upon current resources. Management simultaneously creates its own prioritized list and the desired time for return to service.

In an ideal world, both lists will be very similar. For example, they'll have the items in the same order and the same order of magnitude of return to service. If IT puts the internal Wi-Fi network last and estimates return to service three weeks after a new office is located, but management says 2.5 weeks after the new office is located, they're basically in the same ballpark.

On the other hand, if IT is putting the external VPN last and management is putting it near the top of the list, there's an obvious disconnect.

This is the point where assumptions have to be discussed and goals stated. It is also a place for compromise. Management may be thinking, "As long as we can get the external VPN up and running, people can work from home while we find new office space." IT may be thinking, however, "There's no point in setting up the VPN until we have new file servers and we won't have a location for them until the new office space is located." Neither party is necessarily right. But until they discuss this, they may not realize why the other party is thinking the way that it is.

In addition to the order, the time to restoration is critical. Both parties may agree that having the external API up and running is priority number one. But based on current resources, IT is thinking it's going to take at least 48 hours, because they don't have the extra equipment or a place to put it. They estimate that it's going to take a day to get the proper hardware and a place to locate it, and another day to set up things. They have no budget right now, but they're figuring that during a disaster, they'd get the budget to do this. And perhaps in the past, the budget requests for a hot standby were turned down as too expensive.

Meanwhile, management wants the API back up in 48 minutes. Suddenly, they realize they can't have it both ways: not spending money now, but having near instant failover later.

Of course, while doing the planning, you have to look at it holistically. As I pointed out, ordering file servers without a location to put them does no one much good. This needs to go into the planning. And once a disaster occurs, you can pull out your disaster plan, implement ICS, and get folks fulfilling the Operations, Planing, Logistics, and Finance roles so that everything is handled.

Everything we just discussed is great for large disasters. And honestly, most disaster planning books cover it in more detail.

But what about smaller disasters? Sometimes management's role is to smooth the bumps and play blocker to other distractions.

For example, if there's a major data center meltdown, management may need to tell the salesperson wanting his weekly reports to "hold his horses." While the weekly report may be critical to the salesperson, it is probably not the best use of IT's time right then and there.

During an actual disaster, the roles often reverse. Going back to the lessons from Chapter 3, while someone in management will almost certainly play the role of the Incident Commander, it's very likely that IT personnel will fill the roles of Operations and Planning Chiefs. They'll call the shots—determining what is required, and when, and in what order. It's also quite possible that they'll head up the Logistics Section to make sure that the proper equipment is ordered and delivered to where it needs to be. The Finance Section Chief will almost certainly be a person from management because they can sign the checks. But, again, they'll be working closely with the others in the command structure.

PTSD

Since this is a chapter on management and IT, I want to add a short section on recognizing the impact that a major incident can have on personnel.

Post-traumatic stress disorder is often associated with combat veterans, fire fighters, or police officers who have faced dangerous or deadly situations. But the truth is that it can impact anyone who has had a traumatic experience. While having a disk fail may not be a dangerous or deadly experience, the experience of facing and handling major IT disasters can be traumatic. For example, the IT director may end up feeling personally responsible for the jobs of her fellow employees as a result of the outage.

PTSD may not manifest itself immediately. In fact, it often does not. As part of DR planning and response, management should consider bringing in experienced counselors to aid in PTSD diagnosis and counseling.

It should also be emphasized that experiencing PTSD is *not* a sign of weakness or incompetence. While there's excellent research into the causes and treatment of PTSD, it's clear that it's not as simple as being "weak-willed" or the like. As a manager, you should create an environment where your employees can come to you if they feel they are experiencing PTSD and not feel or risk stigmatization.

Finally, not everyone actually experiences PTSD. In fact, most people never will. If members of your team really do not seem to be experiencing it, that may actually be OK. But if any do, take it seriously.

Real-World Example: Pizza Delivery

Once during a minor incident, my team and I were hunched over our keyboards trying to figure out the problem. The CEO of our company came in and asked a simple question: "Can I order you folks some pizza?"

It was a simple question, but one worthy of discussion here. In a single sentence, he was saying a lot. For one, he was recognizing his own limitations. He wasn't about to sit down at a keyboard and solve the problem. That wasn't his skill. He was recognizing his trust in us. He didn't have to ask for updates or anything because he knew we'd give them when appropriate, and at that moment, our time was best spent on actually debugging and solving the problem. He was also recognizing the time of the day and the amount of time we had spent so far, and would most likely continue to spend on the problem. We were getting hungry and that can honestly get distracting. So he was removing a small but somewhat important barrier to our productivity.

Another example (one most people are familiar with) is that of the "Miracle on the Hudson" flight with Captain Chesley "Sully" Sullenberger and First Officer Jeffrey Skiles. Generally, when pilots are flying commercial aircraft, you hear them requesting permission. They may want to change altitudes or flight paths and will radio air traffic control for permission. ATC will review the request, see what other flights may be impacted, and approve or deny the request. In this case, ATC is controlling or managing all the air traffic.

However, with the words "Mayday, Mayday, Mayday" or something similar, the roles suddenly become reversed. ATC is now in the position of offering suggestions, but the pilot in command has to make the final decisions, and in fact, may make demands of ATC that they normally wouldn't. For example, in the case of the Miracle on the Hudson, ATC offered several suggestions of runways at La Guardia. Normally, a plane wouldn't take that as a suggestion as much as an order as to which runway to land on. This wasn't a normal situation, however, and Captain Sullenberger realized that his aircraft didn't have the energy to make it to La Guardia. Therefore, he did the only thing that he could do for a safe landing: ditch the aircraft in the Hudson River. Unconventional, definitely, but it saved lives.

Analysis

Under normal operations, management directs IT in its duties and goals. In normal operations, ATC tells planes where to fly, where to take off, and where to land.

During a crisis, though, both groups need to be able to swap those roles quickly and recognize their limitations and strengths. My boss couldn't solve the immediate problem, but he could remove one obstacle, hunger, so that we could work more efficiently. ATC couldn't force Captain Sullenberger to land at La Guardia, and once the final result was obvious, ATC was able to alert the proper emergency services to the situation.

Don't be loath to invert or modify the management structure as needed to get the job done.

Recommended Reading

For further information on PTSD, visit http://www.ptsd.va.gov/public/ PTSD-overview/basics/how-common-is-ptsd.asp.

People

I'll state the obvious. Hire the right people and treat them correctly.

OK, that's a pretty boring and short chapter, so let me expand a bit. There are a lot of books out there on how to hire the best person, how to write great résumés and the like. In my experience, a lot of the advice in both departments is pure bunk. Some of my best hires have been on pure gut instinct. Some of my worst hires looked great on paper but didn't pan out at all once things started to get rough.

Let's start with the important point that not everyone has to be a superstar and not everyone you hire necessarily has to be able to able to step up and take command during a crisis. However, they do need to be able to do their job and know what it is.

Hiring the Right Person for the Right Job

The answers to the obvious hiring questions depend on the scale of the crisis and the person's role during a crisis. For example, you may have a person who just simply has the knack for setting up machine after machine for users and can do so hour after hour without getting bored or making mistakes. They're not going to be the person in charge of responding to a major office failure, but you're going to be able to rely on them to build the 250 new machines you're having drop shipped to the new office after the old one burns down.

On the other hand, you may have a person who can keep 50 things in their head at once, has five backup plans formulating in case something goes wrong with the current plan and can juggle four pieces of fruit, all at the same time.

© Greg D. Moore 2016

G. D. Moore, *IT Disaster Response*, DOI 10.1007/978-1-4842-2184-6_7

But if you put them in charge of building 250 new machines, they're going to get bored, make simple mistakes, and start to try to improve the process on the fly and generally make a mess of things. Neither is a better employee than the other, but both need to be recognized for their strengths and weaknesses and put into the proper role during a crisis. And they need to be given the proper resources. If the person building 250 new machines says they need 20 folding tables and four 20-amp circuits to do their job, get it for them and get out of their way.

When I've hired people, I've found it best to try to figure out what I'm really hiring for and to figure out the motivation of the person I'm interviewing.

For example, if the job description is database administrator, am I really looking for someone who can monitor performance, make sure jobs are run, and perhaps write a query or two? Or do I need someone who I know can recover a database and ensure the availability groups and failover are working? When interviewing them I'm going to try to tailor the questions to the goals I've identified.

For me, equally important is motivation. Why do they want this particular job? You'll have to determine for yourself what motivations you find acceptable and make sense. In my experience however, those who are into IT simply for the money are generally the ones you want to avoid. The *why* may also depend on the person involved. One interviewee I had disliked working with people. Had I been hiring for a NOC position where they would have only had to interact with other IT people, they might have been a decent hire. The position I was hiring for was basically a help desk position at a small company where everyone was expected to interact with everyone. He made it clear he preferred if people would just drop off their broken machines, describe the problem and leave. This was not going to work at this particular company.

Retaining the People You Hire

Once you hire your people, keep them. Again, there are books on this subject, but in my experience, it's the little things. If your company has a policy of free soda, don't take it away to save a few dollars. If you have comp time, be lenient and generous with it.

One thing that people often forget about IT is that it's often one of those jobs where failure is not an option. I used to say that it's like baseball. In baseball, a batter who gets a hit one-third of the time is considered a good hitter. In sales, if a salesperson closed 90% of their sales, they'd be considered a great salesperson. If programmers released code that was 99% bug free (and I'll note before any programmers jump on me, I do think that overall the quality of coding has gone up), they'd be doing great. Yet, in IT, if we're doing 99%, that's often considered merely a passing grade. Often we need to be 99.9% or better.

Make sure that your people are content knowing that when things go well, they'll rarely, if ever, get praise. But when something bad happens, the world will look at them.

Ultimately, though, management should not sway hiring. Don't hire the boss's niece unless you'd hire her regardless of the family affiliation.

Hire the best. And hire a person who is going to challenge you and your assumptions when necessary, but get the job done when required.

Also, don't hire the wrong people. I've interviewed people who were technically very competent but were not a good fit for the company. Generally, this should focus on company culture. If your company has a very structured approach to promotions and job duties, and the candidate is someone who feels more comfortable going with the flow and doing what needs to be done without reference to job title, it won't be a good fit for either you or the candidate.

On the other hand, don't be afraid of hiring the candidate who is willing to get into your face—in a respectful manner, of course. In the week-long cave rescue class I help teach, there is a mantra: Is it safe and does it work? Note that there's nothing there about it being the best solution. I once saw a practice rescue get hung up for close to three hours while the advanced students tried to come up with the "best solution." One of the beginner students was frustrated and complained, "We did this at the beginning of the week in 15 minutes!" He was right. And his solution was safe and it worked. But, because the advanced students were caught up in trying to find some mythical "best solution," they wasted two and a half hours. In a real emergency, the instructors would have stepped in and sorted things out. However, it was a great learning experience, which was ultimately the point of the exercise.

But what really needed to happen was for the folks trying to get things done to step back, acknowledge all the viewpoints, and keep their eye on the goal of being safe and making it work. In this case, the goal was to get the mock patient out as quickly and as safely as possible; the goal was not to use a complicated but nice haul system. Having an employee that can get in your face in a respectful manner—and you listening to them—can save the day.

I mentioned free soda. This was a very common perk at many software companies during the first dot-com bubble. It was a cheap perk and the benefit of a highly caffeinated workforce probably didn't hurt.

Then something happened. The bubble burst and companies started to look at costs as their income sources dried up. (Back then, many companies were in a mythical "pre-revenue" stage that many investors were banking on to eventually make them millionaires.) One of the obvious places to cut costs was the soda perk. It seemed simple. Assume your typical employee was drinking two cans of soda a day, which cost you 50 cents apiece, and there were

50 people in your company. That's more than $6,000 a year on soda alone! That could pay for a couple new laptops for your salespeople—and everyone knows you need salespeople to close the sales.

So, it's either two laptops for your sales team—or the soda. So the soda goes.

What happens next, though, is often not measured easily on the books, especially in a smaller startup with less experienced HR people. Your lead developer decides that the company down the street is offering free soda *and* pizza once a week. The free pizza by itself was never really enough of a draw to cause him to quit, but the loss of free soda was. From his point of view, the company has decided that an extra $1/day or about $250/year for him alone is too much. He decides to leave your company. It's not the cost of the soda in his mind—the company can easily cover the cost of soda. It's the principle of the thing.

Now, this developer may have been with your company since day one and he knows the code inside and out. When customer service reports a bug, he can typically find it within a few hours and fix it not long afterward.

Sure, the person you hire to replace him will eventually be at that point. But it typically takes months to get a new hire up to speed. In the meantime, instead of identifying and a fixing a big within a few hours, it now takes a few days. This is an indirect cost that can't necessarily be measured, but does ultimately have an impact on the bottom line.

And let's say that your company uses an outside recruiter. The recruiter finds the perfect hire. Everything checks out. You hire a new person. Then six months after the trial period, the invoice from the recruiter comes. The cost to find that new hire is far higher than the $6K you saved in soda for the year.

And quickly, you realize that this was only the first of many of your staff to leave because of the principle of the soda.[1]

You might be thinking, "Yeah, but people are going to leave no matter what. Why should I care if it's because of soda or not?"

Now consider that suddenly your site goes down. You realize that it's a code issue and you want to get it back up in a hurry, so you call your old lead developer. Even though it might have been soda, how less likely do you think it is that he'll put his heart into solving your problem? Now consider the same person had left on great terms and felt like you really cared about him and his career? How likely do you think he'll be willing to help out?

---

[1]For more thoughts on the matter, see https://steveblank.com/2009/12/21/the-elves-leave-middle-earth-%E2%80%93-soda%E2%80%99s-are-no-longer-free/

Please note that I'm not suggesting you should suddenly go out and start offering free soda to your employees if you don't already. That's not the point. The point is to consider the impacts of removing what are seemingly small perks and how employees are going to react.

What is worse is when one group is treated less favorably than another. How many times does the sales team go out for a great dinner, but when you want to buy your team some take-out food because they're working late, you're told it's not in the budget? When word of this gets to the members of the IT team, it impacts morale.

Another item that you can work on is making sure that your team works no harder than you do. If you're expecting your team to work 50-hour weeks (which, over time, is a bad idea), you should be working 51 hours a week. Your team is looking to you for leadership. If you're not willing to put in the effort, don't expect them to.

I can't emphasize enough the importance of employee retention as part of a good DR plan. While you can bring in new skilled employees, they do not necessarily know the company culture and the company's priorities from day one.[2]

People During a Major Disaster

Let's tie this into a disaster response. If your team doesn't expect morale to be supported during normal operations, they're not going to expect it during a major disaster.

If you've shown them that you're willing to take care of them during normal operations, they're more likely to assume the same during a major disaster.

First, don't burn them out. Your CEO may push you to operate 24/7 for as long as possible to resume normal operations. Don't expect individuals to be able to maintain such a pace for very long. Mistakes will creep in and moods will change. Plan for rehab time. In ICS, teams are generally deployed for specific Operational Periods with time provided to hand-off tasks to other teams. This includes all members of the General Staff. When developing your DR plans, consider options for staff rehab, including food, a place to sleep, and perhaps a separate place to socialize or contact loved ones. You may want to arrange to have a contract in place with a local hotel or motel to house employees during a major disaster. (Of course, consider that if the disaster is large enough, the hotel/motel may not be able to provide the promised resources.)

---

[2]https://www.zanebenefits.com/blog/bid/312123/employee-retention-the-real-cost-of-losing-an-employee

I mentioned providing the ability to contact loved ones. This can be critical. Your goals and needs may not be the same as your employees. While they may be eager to get the company back up and running again, during a major disaster (such as Hurricane Katrina), they may be understandably distracted with worries about their families. You may want to consider in the worst-case scenarios by providing spaces for families to stay. Not only will this allow your employees to focus on the problems in your facility, it will show that your concerns extend beyond the immediate issue.

In addition to the concern for your employees' families, also keep in mind concern for your employees themselves. No company is worth the lives of your employees, especially when it comes to IT disasters. There may be times when you simply have to tell your employees to *stop*. They may suffer from what is called "go fever" and want to do things like charge into the burning data center to grab servers before they are destroyed. This should not be allowed to happen for obvious reasons. But even a more mundane disaster, such as the aftermath of flooding, may require you to slow down or stop your employees from acting. There may be electrical hazards that they're not aware of or even medical hazards such as mold. This is an area where your ICS Safety Officer must have a say in your response.

During a flooding incident (ironically, the HVAC system on the roof failed and sprung a leak), I had to stop employees (who were trying to be helpful) from shutting down computers and servers. While their intentions were good, I didn't think the fact that they were standing in water was worth the risk to them. We ended up shutting down power to the entire floor at the circuit panel box.

As with the smokehouse fire discussed in Chapter 2, the business owner was able to work with the fire department to have a firefighter remove the critical equipment. This is another example where if you have a properly setup ICS, you can work with the fire department's ICS to get things done. While their primary goal is extinguishing the fire, if they have the resources, they may be able to work with you to handle other issues that may be critical. Also, this is yet another reason to contact them before a major incident, so that you can provide them with floor plans and advise them of any potential hazards (such as the fire suppression system in a room that will remove all the oxygen gas) or any requests that you have.

Finally, don't be at all surprised if the quietest, most withdrawn person in your group ends up being the leader you need in the time of crisis and the person who normally stands out in front quietly takes a back seat and ends up being a follower, not a leader.

During training for a cave rescue class, we had one student who during the early part of the week was quiet and didn't necessarily take the lead. Midweek, during one exercise, we heard her clearly and loudly call out, "Stop!" All the students and the instructors stopped what they were doing and waited for her to give further instructions. Suddenly, the other instructors and I realized we weren't the ones being spoken to, but she had quite effectively taken control of the situation, as she should have, and got students refocused on the tasks at hand and made sure things moved along efficiently and expeditiously. She showed the desired and required leadership when it was necessary. On the flip side, some of the loudest, most outgoing people in our classes have been the ones to stand around waiting for instructions when an exercise starts. Don't judge a person by their past actions during normal operations. You may end up being surprised, for the better or for the worse.

ICS and Your People

I once had a mentor sum up the lower levels of ICS to me as follows:

- What is my job?
- Who do I report to?
- Who reports to me?
- How long do I have?
- What resources do I have?

When a disaster strikes and you have to start to manage the people responding, or if you're one of the people responding, keep these five questions in mind.

What is my job? This may sound obvious, but during a disaster, everyone's jobs may completely change and people may not be aware of what they need to do. Classically, this is seen on public streets when someone suffers a medical emergency. One of the first things taught in a first aid or a CPR class is to point to a specific bystander and tell them, "Call 911." This appears to be a trivial example, but often a crowd will form around an injured person with everyone assuming that someone else has called 911. So, during a disaster, make sure specific people have a specific job. Don't vaguely suggest, "Someone should restore the data." Tell the person whose job it is to restore the data to do so. And if you're the one told to restore the data, make sure that you fully understand what is required. Does this mean all the data, including the archival data? Is the request only for database data? Is there specific data that should be restored first? Know and fully understand what is being asked of you.

Who do I report to? After telling a person what to do, make sure they know who they report to. Will it be you or someone else? The person can get the job done, but getting the job done is useless if they don't know who to report to about the status of the job. This is also important because if this person encounters obstacles and can't restore the data, they know who to go to for additional guidance. If you're the one being told to do something, make sure that you know who to report to when you have issues or the job is complete.

Who reports to me? If you're appointing a team, make sure that the leader knows who is on their team. If you're appointed to lead a team, make sure that you know who is on your team. Again, don't let things be vague. If your manager says, "Oh, someone will help you restore the data," dig in your heels and insist on knowing who that will be.

How long do I have? This is more critical than it sounds. For one thing, you need to know if the timeframe is realistic. If they ask you to restore 2 terabytes of data in the next 30 minutes, you will most likely have to push back and say that it's not possible. On the flipside, you may be told, "You've got 24 hours to get this done," but you know it only takes 12 hours. This permits you to gauge your response, perhaps temper things a bit, and tell your other team members they don't have to race in to help you.

What resources do I have? Again, a critical question to ask and to make sure is answered. Don't ask the impossible of your team. If you ask them to restore 2 terabytes and there's only 1 terabyte of disk space, you can't do your job. Or if you're asked to build 250 desktops and you only have one person your team, or you have 20 people but only desk space for four desktops at a time, you can't complete your job. As a manager, don't set up your team to fail. Provide them the resources that they need. If you can't provide the resources, change the job to fit the resources available.

Perhaps you're reading this and thinking that ICS really isn't much different from any other style of employee management. You're right. Part of the purpose of ICS is exactly that: to provide a management system during a disaster. Hopefully, you'll find that your management system is not very different during normal operations and during a disaster.

Real-World Example: Hires at My First Startup

Back in the heyday of the first Internet dot-com bubble, I managed to find some excellent hires.

Our company was just starting up and I had the budget for a single IT person. We had a basic job description, but we were growing so quickly that a big part of the job description was the cliché "other duties as assigned."

I conducted four or five interviews one day. Several of the candidates were not a good fit. It was pretty obvious. But two of them stood out. Both were solid candidates. One had a degree in teaching. She was looking to make a career change. The other had no formal degree, but lots of experience in troubleshooting.

Fortunately, we were in high-growth mode, so I went to my manager with the conundrum. He had a simple answer: "Hire them both."

To this day, they were among the best hires I have made. There were a few others I added to the IT team over time. Two other members of this team stand out. One was a former EMT who had responded to the TWA Flight 800 crash over Long Island Sound. Another was a former optometrist.

In another case, I interviewed a candidate who was an excellent in all ways. She was technically competent, would have been a pleasure to work with, and would make a great addition to the team. However, I was hesitant to hire her and was thankful when she actually pulled herself out of the running. What was it that made her a bad fit? Ultimately, it was the company. We were a small, fast-paced company that was growing quickly in a horizontal fashion, but not vertically. This meant that while she'd learn a lot and contribute a lot, there was no clear career path at the company for her. This was true for pretty much all of us. However, it was clear that this was important to her. This didn't make her right or wrong. It simply made our company a bad fit for her. She later accepted an offer at GE, where the corporate culture was a far better fit for her. I've always wondered how far up she's moved and if GE knew how lucky they were to get her.

Analysis

The teacher ended up heading up the internal IT department and brought order out of the chaos that's standard at a startup company. She wasn't so much into the 24/7 operations side, but that was fine because she built the internal IT department and ended up managing it several years later.

When I hired the former EMT, I told him that one day he'd walk into my office, close the door, and tell me he had found a better job. Sure enough, after a couple of years, he walked into my office, closed the door, and told me he had found a better job. I asked him for details. I then said that I could talk to HR about a counter offer, but that quite frankly, he'd be a fool to not take the other offer. The reality was that at the time, our company didn't have positions for him to grow into. The other offer included free college tuition—something I knew we couldn't match. But, he was leaving on great terms, not because we had cut the soda. I knew that I could contact him if anything went wrong later—and he'd return my call.

On the other hand, I had a hire that I knew the instant he decided to leave the job. I walked into the NOC and noticed that the graphs seemed a bit "off." Yes, that's the very technical term for something that just doesn't seem right. There was nothing obvious and no alarms were going off, but the CPU usage was a tad higher than we should have been seeing. I mentioned to him that something wasn't right. He replied that everything was working and no alarms were going off, so everything was fine.

Technically he was right, but that wasn't really the response I wanted. I really wanted to know what was different and why. I don't know if I was overly tired or just having a bad day, but I snapped at him. And I snapped at him loudly enough that folks outside the NOC heard me chewing him out. In the middle of trying to get my point across, I saw a look cross his eyes. I knew right then that he had, rightly, lost his respect for me. I had just belittled him in front of others for seemingly no good reason.

During the next shift, I made a point to apologize to him in front of others. I was hoping to retrieve some modicum of respect from him by admitting my mistake in front of the folks that I had embarrassed him in front of.

But it was too late. Three weeks later he had found another job and gave notice.

People are not like machines that can be swapped in and out like hard drives. Work to develop your teams. Pay attention to the little things that build morale.

The Small Stuff

There are no big problems. There are just a lot of little problems."

—Henry Ford

In Chapter 1, I defined a disaster as an unplanned interruption in business that has an adverse impact on finances or other resources.

I used the example of a printer running out of paper as a very minor example of this. It doesn't sound like much, but it's not planned and has a negative impact on time as someone has to recognize and respond to the issue.

In Chapter 3, I provided a tool of managing disasters: ICS. Let's start by applying ICS to the case of a printer running out of paper.

You're sitting at the helpdesk when a user calls in and says the printer isn't working. You look at the print queue in question and realize the printer is out of paper. Fortunately, this is an easy solution. You go the supply room, grab a ream of paper, crack it open, load the printer, and tell the person that their printout will be ready in a few minutes.

While in the supply room, you noticed that the paper supply is getting low, so you go to person in charge of supplies and ask them to order another case or two of printer paper.

Ten minutes after the initial phone call the "disaster" is over and you can go back to playing *Fallout 4* on the company LAN (OK, hopefully you're not doing that).

Was this a disaster? Based on the definition in Chapter 1, yes. But I prefer to call this an *incident*, mostly because *disaster* is such a loaded term.

© Greg D. Moore 2016
G. D. Moore, *IT Disaster Response*, DOI 10.1007/978-1-4842-2184-6_8

Also, as soon as we think incident, we should think about applying the Incident Command System discussed in Chapter 3. The key here is to remember that ICS describes functions, not specific roles. You don't need to spin up a huge command structure to handle a tiny incident. In this case, **you** are the entire ICS.

- Incident Commander: Check. You have the authority to make the decisions and to make sure that they're carried out.

- Planning Section Chief: Pretty clear what the plan is. Put more paper in the printer.

- Operations Section Chief: You're the one putting the paper in the printer.

- Logistics Section Chief: Again, you're the one getting the materials required to solve the problem. In this case, it's simply walking to the supply closet, getting more paper, and putting it into the printer. However, you're smart enough to plan ahead and tell someone to order more paper. You can think of this as one ICS structure interacting with another—that is, two Logistics people planning ahead. Such interaction is allowed under ICS and is in fact encouraged. (Because, imagine what would happen if you went to the supply closet and there was no paper.)

- Finance Section Chief: Well, the total cost of the incident itself was a few minutes of your time, which is covered in your salary. So you really don't have to do much here, other than perhaps log your time.

- Safety Officer: Other than the possibility of a paper cut, this is pretty routine.

That's it. You've got all the roles covered. This is an extreme example and you may be asking the point of claiming that ICS covers this. That's a fair question. And the answer is that invoking ICS gets you in to a specific mode of thinking. Once you start to think about ICS for the smaller problems, it becomes second nature for the larger problems.

Imagine what might happen if you go to the supply room and there is no paper? The incident now has become larger because in part, you have the original person immediately impacted, but also because you know that soon other printers may be in the same empty state and you won't be able to handle that as easily as you might like. Without paper, your company's business may come to a standstill.

Or you discover a full case of printer paper on a top shelf that weighs more than 50 lbs. And you barely weigh twice that. Getting that paper may in fact be a safety hazard that you have to account for.

Or, it might be the error message was inaccurate and it is really the paper tray sensor that is on the fritz. The printer is full of paper, but thinks it is empty. Now you may need to bring in a repair person or start looking at buying a new printer.

What if the printer is at a remote office and you have to direct someone local to put paper in it. Now your ICS structure, specifically the Operations Section, has expanded.

Another reason to use ICS is because a small incident can quickly become a large one and spiral out of the ability of a single person to control it. As mentioned in Chapter 3, ICS was developed in response to a major forest fire in California that killed 16 people. But keep in mind that every large forest fire begins as a small one. The goal of a quick response to a forest fire is to keep it from becoming a larger one. But, by adopting ICS from the get-go, if the fire does explode in size, the same response structure can simply be expanded as needed rather than replaced.

An unfortunately all-too-common incident these days is so-called ransomware. If you're not familiar with this term, you should familiarize yourself with it. Basically, it is a computer worm that usually enters via some sort of Trojan horse program. Generally, it sits in the background, encrypting files on the hard drive until suddenly it pops up a message that says something like what's shown in Figure 8-1.

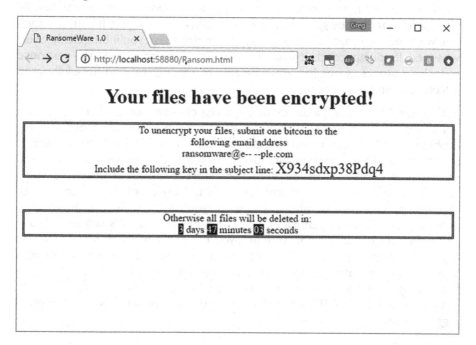

Figure 8-1. Ransomware encryption message

Imagine that you're sitting at the helpdesk first thing in the morning and Paul from finance calls up and reads this screen to you.

So far, it's just one person. But you're smart enough to know that on the network, this probably means you will be getting a lot of calls rather quickly. You're also familiar enough with ransomware to know that it's probably too late: most files on your network were encrypted in the background days ago. So, while this is an isolated incident and might remain that way, in the back of your mind, you have to start to think about how large you may have to expand your response.

You might be lucky. It might be only this individual's computer that is infected. If that's the case, you again are the sum total of the ICS response.

After looking at it for an hour, you might realize that all the finance department computers are infected and the virus has spread to the network, but only the finance files are impacted. You decide to spin up the response to include three or four more people from the IT department, but that's all you need.

Or, you realize that the CFO had sent out an email that included the virus. Now it's an all-hands on-deck response that will probably involve senior management. The CFO is not only the victim of the disaster, but is now probably filling the role of Finance Section Chief.

So, what may start (and hopefully remain) a small incident that you can handle by yourself, can quickly grow beyond your ability to manage it. If you approach this with the idea that you can handle the entire thing, you'll be quickly overwhelmed. If you approach it with the idea that you can expand the response to include others as needed, you'll be able to react faster and hopefully keep it from growing out of control.

In Chapter 12, we'll talk a bit about the Swiss cheese theory of accidents. But here I want to emphasize that rarely does a big problem start out as a big problem. A 1,000-acre forest fire doesn't start as a 1,000-acre forest fire. It starts with a single cigarette butt being tossed out a window or a campfire that was not fully extinguished. When you start to look at IT problems, you'll soon learn that most start as small problems. Many times, if you can address the small problems while they're still small, you can keep them from growing into larger problems. If you can catch the campfire while it's still smoldering and before it's become a one-acre fire, you can put it out with a pail of water. If you can catch it as a one-acre fire, you can perhaps put it out yourself with a few gallons of water. If you can catch it before it as it becomes a 100-acre fire, a single fire department and a couple of trucks might be able to handle it. Once it becomes a 1000-acre fire or a 10,000 acre fire, you need a much bigger response.

However, the critical thing to keep in mind, is that by using the tools in this book, such as ICS, the response will remain the same regardless of the scale of the disaster. For a 100-acre fire, ICS may consist of a fire chief and two teams for two separate pieces of equipment. The chief may be performing all the roles of ICS at that point, but not necessarily. By the time the fire has grown to 1,000 or 10,000 acres, the fire chief has either handed off ICS to someone above him, or he may have adopted a unified command with other chiefs and have a full-staffed incident command center directing hundreds of people in the field.

However, it all started with ICS. The command structure hasn't changed, simply expanded in scope. This is analogous to how your response to ransomware may have expanded as the disaster grew.

Real-World Example: Lost Caving Party

Many years ago, I was part of a large caving group that decided to go to one of the local caves that we usually take beginners to.

Because of the size of the group and the size of the cave, we broke up the larger group into three smaller groups. Two groups went in the main entrance and the third group went into one of the other entrances that joined the main cave via a tight side passage. Our plan was to meet the third group in the cave and then split up again with some folks exiting via the main entrance and others leaving via a third, very wet exit.

I led my group from the main entrance of the cave (which is approximately midway between the two ends of the cave, one end has a small pool and the other end is the very wet exit) to the end with the pool. We then headed back toward the very wet exit. Along the way, we never encountered the third group that was supposed to come in via the side passage from their entrance.

We thought this unusual, but not impossible. A matter of timing could simply mean that they took longer than expected to enter and get down the side passage.

After leading my group through the wet exit, we were outside the cave, dripping wet and cold. I proceeded to check with the leader of the second party to see if he had encountered the third group at all. He also had not seen them. Now I was getting worried.

I immediately went into rescue mode and formulated a plan. This was still a small incident and I hoped it would remain that way. At that time, I was fulfilling all the roles of ICS. I selected a strong caver and we proceeded to go in via the wet exit and go all the way to the other end and come back. We assumed that we'd find the third group and learn what was going on. The plan was to travel light and fast and to not search any of the side passages.

This was the first, and to date, the only time I've gone in via the wet exit. Putting my sopping wet caving clothing back on was not the most pleasant experience of my life. But, because we were moving quickly, I warmed up. We got to the far end of the cave and turned around, now completely confused because there was no sign of the third party. Given my experience in that cave, I figured there was no way they could still be entering the cave via the side passage. I figured they had either exited by the main entrance and we had simply missed them because of timing, or they were somehow lost in a section of the cave that we had overlooked.

We exited through the wet exit and I gathered with the other leaders. This small incident was quickly becoming a large incident. It wasn't simply an over-due party, it was now a lost party. In addition, we knew a member of the party was diabetic and my concern was that this was going to quickly become a lost party with a medically compromised patient.

At this point, the incident had grown beyond my ability to perform all the roles of ICS by myself. Quickly, I started to spread out the roles of ICS. I made someone the Logistics Chief. This person made plans to gather more light sources (this was so long ago that we were still using carbide lamps) and also to get extra food so that we could treat the diabetic party member if needed.

I worked with the Planning Chief to identify a search plan and to alert 911.

The person who would have become Operations Chief was listening to determine how many search teams we should have and who would be on them.

Just as we were getting ready to put this plan into action, we saw a line of lights coming out of the woods. The lost party had returned.

Analysis

Briefly, the third party had taken longer than expected to come in via the side entrance. This was due to it being tight and one of the members getting stuck. They managed to get unstuck and continued on into the cave. By now, we had already gone by the side passage twice, once toward the far end of the cave and once on the way back toward the wet exit.

The leader of the third group had told me he wasn't sure where the main entrance was, but we thought he'd run into my group or the second group and then be told where it was, or he'd find it himself. But because of the delay due to the stuck caver, this never happened.

By the time I did my search sweep, the leader had decided since he couldn't find the main entrance, he would lead his group out of the side entrance. This is why we never saw them during my search sweep. They had already gone back into the side passage to leave the cave.

During the time we were expanding our Incident Command Structure, they were exiting the cave. They came out of the woods just as we were about to put plans into action.

If, however, they had gotten stuck again or something had happened in the tight side passage, we would have carried out our plan. And if we had called 911 and the sheriff's department had shown up, we would have handed off ICS to them.

This started out as a small incident: an overdue caving party. It grew into a larger incident: a missing caving party. It was on its way to growing into an even larger incident: a missing caving party with a medical injury. We didn't wait for it to grow larger; we responded to the incident when it was still small. Had it become a much larger incident, we would have already had the required parts of a proper response in place and been able to hand it off to the even larger ICS that the sheriff's department would put into place.

Make a point of adopting ICS for even the most trivial incidents. You don't have to make a huge deal out of it. Note that in the examples given, there wasn't really any formal paperwork, meetings, or the like. Simply, people adopted their roles or were appointed roles as needed. But had the incidents grown much larger, such as with the ransomware, ICS would have continued to work.

I will also note that when we teach our cave rescue classes, we often use ICS throughout the entire week so that our students get much more comfortable with the concept of it and it becomes second nature to them.

In the next chapter, we'll talk about larger disasters.

The Big Stuff

As I mentioned earlier, when companies think of disasters, they often think of the big things: fires, floods, major server crashes. Those things do in fact happen. Entire books are written about just these sorts of disasters. I'm only going to spend a single chapter on them.

First, it should be noted that many businesses do not survive a major disaster. In 2010, the Gartner Group said only 6% of companies survive two years after a major data loss.[1]

That should be a very sobering thought for any company. Is your company going to be the part of the 6% or the 94%?

I've been very fortunate. In my career spanning more than 20 years, I've only worked with two companies that suffered a major disaster. In the first case, their facility was the victim of arson. The company survived, fortunately. In the second case, the SAN suffered a major meltdown. Again, the company was fortunate to survive, but it was close.

I said this wasn't going to be your typical "how-to" book on disasters and it won't be. I will discuss several topics here that may help you be in that 6%.

First, as I've said throughout this book: have a plan. You don't have to specify every detail. The quote by Helmuth Graf von Moltke, "No battle plan ever survives contact with the enemy," is very apt here.

---

[1]http://www.homelandsecuritynewswire.com/gartner-only-6-percent-companies-survive-longer-two-years-after-losing-data

© Greg D. Moore 2016
G. D. Moore, *IT Disaster Response*, DOI 10.1007/978-1-4842-2184-6_9

You need to have a very general plan, a set of goals, and then the ability to execute operations to get toward that goal as things change. I discussed this a bit with airplane crashes in Chapter 4. The goal of any pilot remains the same: to get the plane on the ground in one piece with all souls on board still alive. But the plan may change second to second as the situation changes. Right before the Sioux City crash, the pilots were directed to Runway 31. Unfortunately, due to their situation, they realized that they couldn't line up to Runway 31 in time and were lined up to Runway 22, a shorter runway that was also closed and had the emergency equipment lined up on it. The pilots told the airport they had no choice but to try for Runway 22. Immediately, the ground plans were changed for the new reality and emergency equipment moved. Had they stuck with their original plan of landing on Runway 31, they most likely would have lost the aircraft and all souls on board.

Second, IT specific, you need to have backups! And make sure that they're readable and available during your disaster. This sounds like it doesn't need to be said, but more often than not when I talk to various IT folks about their incidents, an all too common refrain is, "Well, we thought we had backups." Or in one case, "Well, we had backups, but they couldn't be read."

The latter reason can happen for a variety of reasons. In one case, a company had set up their backup software incorrectly and each time they thought they were doing an actual backup, the backup system was actually executing a "mock backup" that exercised the tape unit and software, but didn't actually write anything. I've also heard of cases where the tape system was so old that restoring data from the tapes took days or weeks in tracking down hardware that could actually do the job. In one specific case, a client of mine successfully read and wrote their backups, but their major DR plan included shifting operations to a remote facility. It turned out that despite the software and hardware recommendations from the staff at the remote facility, the client's tapes could not be read at the remote facility. This meant that one of the most key parts of their disaster recovery plan could not be executed in a timely manner.

In a large-scale disaster, you almost certainly want to take advantage of something like ICS. You will need some sort of management structure that probably does not exactly correspond to the normal running of the business. You may need to run your ICS parallel to running your business. While your core facilities may be unavailable and most normal business operations cannot be performed, other operations may be required.

For example, if your salespeople normally work on the road and work remotely, they may be minimally impacted by a major disaster and their management structure may stay intact and continue operating.

However, if you're normally manufacturing a product and your facilities are destroyed, you may need to continue to have your buyers work with vendors and arrange for shipment to a standby location or the like. In the case of the smokehouse fire discussed in Chapter 2, as the fire department was performing their mop-up operations, a delivery truck full of fresh meat pulled into the delivery lot. Plans had to be quickly made to accept the meat and do something with it.

Many businesses often undergo office moves over the course of their lifetime. A proper office move can take a year or more to effectively perform. This may include items such determining a location, renovating it, installing the required desks and IT infrastructure, and then the actual move itself.

During a major incident, you may need to compress everything into a few days. On top of that, you may have to consider that the facility you move into will almost certainly be temporary. This means once the initial incident is handled and things settled down, your personnel will need to start to gear up for another major operation.

Also, a major incident often causes several days of highly intensive operations with people functioning on less sleep than normal. As discussed in Chapter 7 (and worth reviewing), this can cause a number of impacts. Tempers may flare over seemingly trivial things. People make more mistakes. And sometimes people simply drop out as exhaustion overtakes them. A key part to handling a major incident is managing the people. This may mean imposing mandatory rest periods on key personnel. This may seem to prolong the incident, but will probably make it shorter because people coming back from a rest period are typically more refreshed, more productive, and less prone to making mistakes that may make the ongoing incident worse.

Another major issue during a major incident is that key documents may simply be unavailable. The company checkbook may not be available and vendors responding in an emergency may want to be paid right away (in part because they know the survival rates of companies and are afraid there won't be any-one around six months later to pay them).

Other documents, such as incorporation papers, may be unavailable until new copies can be obtained.

Key personnel may be injured or dead. In at least one incident that I'm famil-iar with, the CEO and CFO, the only two people with signing authority for a small company, were killed in a car accident. So while the company itself didn't directly suffer a disaster, the resulting fallout of having no one available to sign checks nearly bankrupted the company.

To sum up much of this, you have to look at a major incident holistically— not just the incident. The fire may have been put out or the flood waters have receded, but that's just the tip of the iceberg. If you are simply focused on the fire or the water, you will miss the larger picture.

As a result, when crafting a disaster or business continuity plan, you should think of everything that could go wrong and how it would impact the plan itself. I had a client whose plan involved failing over operations to a corporate data center. At one point, the corporate IT folks upgraded the VPN solution to use a soft-token emailed to the employee's email account. It didn't dawn on me for a few days, but this was a potentially a huge issue if they had a disaster. In almost any case that they would have to failover to their corporate data center, their mail server would be unavailable until after the failover was complete. However, they would not be able to get into the data center to start the mail failover until they had received their emailed VPN soft-tokens. It was a bit of a catch-22. Fortunately, it turned out there was no requirement for the VPN soft-token to go to a corporate address. As such, I advised them (and did so with my account) to have the VPN token go to a secure non-corporate account. While other work-arounds existed, they would have been time-consuming.

While that particular issue was unique, the ability to do things like contact your DNS provider or other vendors may be compromised because you may not be able to access email until you can execute certain infrastructure changes. And you may not be able to easily execute such changes until you can handle email.

At a much larger scale, earthquake or hurricane damage can cause your company to face even larger hurdles. These hurdles include the lack of basic services. A power outage over a block or two may be a major disaster for your company, but as long as you have access to fuel for your generators, you should be able to keep the business running. You do have a generator, right? Has it been tested? And by tested I don't mean just turning it on, but actually transferring power to it or setting up a resistance load to test it? As an aside, in a memorable incident at a company I worked for, we failed over to the UPS and the generator started to kick in. However, before the generator was fully operational, the main power came back on, and all the servers lost power. Apparently, the test for the automatic transfer for the UPS/generator had been performed, but no one had bothered to test the automatic failback from the UPS/generator.

But what happens when the infrastructure to deliver the fuel no longer exists, such as after Hurricane Katrina or a major earthquake? Or when higher-priority clients need to get fuel before you do?

In addition, your employees may not be able to make it to your facilities. They may be dealing with emergencies at home.

Consider a disaster event on the scale of Hurricane Katrina in New Orleans. In that case, everything that I mentioned occurred. There were no basic services available for days or weeks. People were displaced, and in many cases, more worried about basic survival than work.

When developing your disaster plan, consider the worst-case scenario and whether you can survive it. It may be too big of a hurdle to plan for.

What this means in some cases is that your plan is simply to do nothing.

Consider a financial institution that handles millions of dollars of money a day. They absolutely should have a plan that includes geographically redundant data centers (perhaps on separate coasts) that won't be impacted by a single disaster. They may even want to contract with hotels to house key personnel *and* their families for the length of a disaster.

But if you run a mom-and-pop business, your best plan may simply be to assume that during a full-scale disaster, you'll shutdown, preserve what you can, high-tail it to safe ground, and wait until you can go back to your facilities and see what insurance will cover. (By the way, now is a good time to call your insurance agent and find out what exceptions there are to your insurance. For example, you might find out that you're covered for water damage due to a hurricane, but only a hurricane. Your insurance company may claim that you need separate flood insurance for damage caused by water. Yes, this has happened.)[2]

Finally, keep things in perspective. As important as it is to try to continue a business, ultimately people are more important. Don't ask people to stay behind during a major weather event to keep the business going if you're going to put their lives at undue risk. Don't ask more of your employees than you might ask of yourself. And keep in mind that most of your employees have families. Do not to ask them to decide between the business and their families.

Real-World Example: One Good, One Bad

In this section, I'll actually discuss two examples. I was personally involved in both. The first illustrates how well a failover can go when things have been tested and everyone is up to speed. The second shows how a lack of planning can lead to a disaster being worse than it would have been otherwise.

Also, in other chapters, the examples often focus on the successful application of the topic discussed in the chapter. This chapter is different. The first example is actually a DR test, not an actual event. The second example shows how bad luck, lack of planning, and not using ICS turned what should have been a decent-sized disaster into an even bigger one.

---

[2]http://www.nydailynews.com/new-york/insurers-sandy-victims-covered-hurricanes-not-floods-article-1.1206785

In the first case, I had been working with a particular client for over two years, helping them build out their DR solution. Due to corporate requirements, there were certain hurdles we had to overcome concerning things like firewall security. However, with a lot of hard work and planning, we managed to overcome the hurdles. I worked closely with the development and QA teams to ensure that we had a viable plan.

Per corporate policy, we were required to perform an annual test to failover to the secondary data center. This may sound like an obvious requirement, but in my experience, very few companies actually mandate an actual test; they just have a plan and assume that everything will go well when the time comes.

This company had several key components that had to be successfully failed over: web services, several key databases, file services, and a few other items. I was mostly in charge of the databases, but was aiding in pretty much everything else.

By September, we set a date for mid-November to perform the failover test. So we waited. Oh wait, no we didn't. What we did was exercise many of the lessons suggested throughout this book. We discussed who would be calling the shots (in this case, the QA manager) and who would be doing what. We also took the time to test individual components. For example, we did several test runs of the file replication service so that we had an idea of the possible latency in the system. This let us revise our DR plan and test to reflect the reality of the system in place.

One of the more complex steps was switching the databases over from a testing setup to the DR setup. Although this was fairly simple, a matter of renaming databases and applying the latest transaction logs, I ran through it several times until I had an easily reproducible script that I could run without error.

We actually practiced several of the other processes until they too had easily reproducible scripts and were done several times without error.

About four days before the actual DR test, we performed our own run-through without the outside auditor watching. It ran very smoothly and we confirmed details, such as how long certain steps would take and in what order they should occur.

Finally, on the day of the scheduled test, the outside auditor observed our test and confirmed that we hit the set benchmarks and proven that the written DR plan would in fact work. It was a successful test with no issues that stood out.

This gave us great confidence that if an actual disaster befell the company, everyone would be able to respond appropriately and continue their business with only minimal interruption. And to be honest, in over 25 years in the industry, I think that this is the first company or client I've worked with that had this level of proven confidence in their DR plan.

In the second case, I was an employee at a major SaaS company. In fact, I was a manager of the IT department and had effectively become a manager of the division in question. For various reasons, we had to move our data center infrastructure. The company had recently acquired this infrastructure. (I, in fact, had been part of the infrastructure and product line that had been acquired.)

One thing that was lacking (for a variety of reasons) was a robust backup architecture of the databases and files in the data center. Mostly this was due to the previous owners' lack of budget. It was a fact that I had never been happy with, but I had very little luck in changing.

Also, due to lack of investment by the previous owners, some of the equipment was starting to display various issues—including the SAN, on which live files were kept, and the NAS devices, where backups were kept.

I had already managed two successful data center migrations, so I wasn't overly worried about this third one. I should have been. It cost me my job and nearly destroyed the company.

During the actual move, when we started to bring up the SAN, various LUNs started to display errors. This had happened before, but everything had resolved itself. But this time, there were more LUNs displaying errors than we had previously seen.

In addition, due to a hurried process, rather than performing a clean shutdown of one of the NAS units, one of the employees simply pulled the plug on it. This left the file system a complete mess. Among other items, this file system contained the near-line backups of many of the files on the SAN.

In retrospect, a number of mistakes were made. My manager and I discussed things very briefly before he became my former manager. Essentially, we ignored several elements of preparation.

We didn't have good backups like we should have.

We didn't allocate the time that we really needed.

We didn't allocate the proper personnel, so that when things *did* go wrong, we rushed into solutions and made mistakes that made things worse.

And because the merger was recent, the new management and my staff and I weren't fully on the same page. We had not yet built up the trust levels in each other's judgment as we should have. As my former manager and I talked about it afterward, I should have asked for more resources and time, and he should have been more forceful in getting me to commit to what was properly needed. I had felt a bit of a need to prove that we could do this migration and I didn't want to burden the new company with too many requests for resources and money.

In addition, because of our different approach to problems, we didn't have a clear management system set up for a proper response. I was trying to use ICS and they were using their own structure. This led to several false starts because we sometimes duplicated recovery efforts, or they would start efforts without looping me into them.

This is really where an ounce of prevention could have a provided a pound of cure.

Ultimately, two seemingly unrelated failures compounded to make a far worse failure. This combined with a less than ideal response, drew out the recovery process and possibly actually caused more data loss than would have happened otherwise.

In reality, no plan would have anticipated the combination of failures. But a good plan would have anticipated at least one of the failures and taken steps to protect against it. And had we had more experience working together, a better managed response would have been possible.

Example Analysis

In the first case, the company did what more companies should do. They didn't just hope and pray, they had a DR plan. They didn't write one and simply put it on the shelf to be pulled down when needed and hoped it worked. They actively built it, tested it, and refined it until they had a very high confidence that it would work.

I'll point out too that the corporate rules required annual testing. This is an important detail because while companies often like to think that things haven't changed that much, in reality, sometimes even small changes can have large ramifications on your DR plans. Without annual or more frequent testing, a DR plan loses value over time.

For example, since the initial DR test was done, the network performance between the two data centers improved. Overall, this was a good thing. On the other hand, the ability to access the VPN in the secondary data center had completely changed. This meant that the previous plan was outdated and that a majority of the employees would need new training and instructions on how to access the backup data center. In addition, some functionality at the database level had changed over the ensuing year.

It was only by performing an annual review of the DR plan and setting a test date that these differences were found.

In the second case, a *lot* of hard work managed to recover most of the data. But it did cost the company thousands of dollars and me many hours of sleep (for about a week, I was sleeping about four hours a night) and it eventually cost me my job. The company survived, however. A bit of luck and a lot of hard work.

Unlike most of the examples in the other chapters, this is probably best described as a counterexample. This incident relied more on luck than it should have.

Good disaster planning should mitigate as many risks as possible and eliminate luck as a factor as much as possible. In Chapter 11, I continue to discuss the importance of testing your disaster plans in nearly real-world scenarios.

When Is a Disaster Response Plan Not Enough?

"No battle plan ever survives contact with the enemy."

—Helmuth von Moltke

So, you've written yourself a DR plan. You have details on how backups will be made. You've determined what systems are critical. You've written down the phone numbers of the people to call. You're all set! Right?

Wrong!

You may have a plan, but you really don't know if it will work.

By analogy to the opening quote, no DR plan survives its first encounter with a disaster.

© Greg D. Moore 2016

G. D. Moore, *IT Disaster Response*, DOI 10.1007/978-1-4842-2184-6_10

First, you need to go through your DR plan and look for critical dependencies that you may have missed. Does recovering the SharePoint server rely on your single SharePoint expert? What happens if he's not available, either due to vacation or due to the incident making him unavailable?

Does your email service rely on you repointing your DNS to a new data center with a different IP, but you need your email address to verify DNS changes?

Will the people who can authorize capital purchases be available? Better yet, will they authorize purchases? You don't want to surprise your CFO with a request to buy $100,000 worth of hardware because your building was flooded. Make sure that before that happens, your CFO is aware of the scale of requests you may make and that she can actually deliver on them. It may be that the company has a line of credit or insurance available they can tap into immediately. Or, it may be that the company doesn't, and your review of the DR plan with senior management may be the first time they've been told such money may be necessary in a very short period of time.

Your plan may recommend that key personal be put up at hotel rooms near the office (or other locations) during a major incident. Will management back this and pay those expenses? Are contracts in place before the disaster occurs? Do you know who gets priority on rooms if multiple companies have similar contracts with that hotel and the same disaster impacts all of them?

This is just a sampling of dependencies you need to think about. Take each step and ask key people what resources they may need to carry out that step, or what resources they may be asked to carry out after that step. Use your ICS model as an example and determine who will most likely be filling each role. Then go to each person and ask them what they would need to carry out that step or what would be needed from them to carry out after that step. Then ask their backups.

Second, who determines when to activate the DR plan? This most likely will depend on the scale of the incident. Going back to our examples, if a printer is out of paper, not only don't you really need a written DR plan, you probably can have almost anyone replace the paper. But, even then, perhaps because of stock re-ordering or a quirky printer, you only want specific people to replace the paper. In that case, even though it's a minor incident, you still need to make it clear who has the authority and who doesn't. But, since we're really talking about larger scale incidents, the sort that do in fact need a written plan, this becomes even more critical.

I don't have a firm metric here, but I recommend that anything that impacts an entire department or more, probably needs authorization to come from a department head or higher. A second metric would be the scale of the disruption. For example, if a department SharePoint server fails, the department head should be the one who can determine if the DR plan should be activated. If the failover can be done seamlessly, then perhaps they don't need to be informed at all, the failover can be performed by someone in IT and then the department head informed. But, if the failover requires for example, a failover to a server in a different facility and people will need to change how they do work, then the department head should almost certainly be involved from the get go.

Thirdly, who is in charge?

Chapter 4 started with a quote from Alexander Haig: "I'm in control here."

If you recall, back in Chapter 4, we discussed CRM and how Captain Sullenberger clearly stated, "My aircraft." He had the authority to do so. In theory, so did First Officer Skiles, but in general, the senior pilot will take command of the aircraft.

However, anyone who knows much about the constitutional line of succession realizes that Alexander Haig wasn't really in line to take over after Reagan at the time. He was by many roundly mocked for that statement. But the truth is that he wasn't trying to exert a constitutional authority he didn't have. He knew and understood that Vice President Bush most likely had the full legal authority if an executive decision came up. He was rather trying to allay fears that the White House was rudderless and that no one could make certain organizational decisions while Vice President Bush was in flight. The reality is, given modern communications, had decisions requiring executive authority been required, Alexander Haig would not have been the one making them. He was referring more to decisions such as making sure the National Security Council was being briefed and that staffers were given enough information to carry out their duties while the White House waited for Vice President Bush to return or for President Reagan to exit surgery.

This may in fact be similar to how your DR plan unfolds. The CEO may declare that the DR plan should be activated, but delegate operational authority to someone else, such as the VP of IT or the like.

Or, someone in your IT department may declare a disaster and start activation of the DR plan. They may even begin to execute portions of the disaster plan before transferring control over to the proper person.

This is true in the real world. If a police officer sees a tanker truck crash and then spill chemicals on the highway, that officer will declare it a disaster and immediately perform the appropriate roles of ICS, including that of Incident Commander. They will transfer authority to someone further up the command chain as necessary as the scope of the accident enlarges. If the accident never progresses beyond perhaps a simple fender-bender with no tank spill or injuries, they may retain their role as Incident Commander.

In corporate terms, the CEO might be fulfilling the role of the Authority Having Jurisdiction and the role of Incident Commander. More likely though, the IC will be a person who is better versed in the IT infrastructure and the protocols for responding. This might be the CIO or Director of IT, for example.

This person then may retain authority, or give a great deal of decision making authority to a qualified Operations Chief.

This is in fact how it has worked cave rescues I've been on have. The Incident Commander has told me or my co-captain essentially, "go get them out." We still would run major decisions by them, but generally the delegation works well.

But, going back to earlier discussions, it is vital that it's clear who is in charge and what level of authority they actually have.

In the case of one DR plan I was asked to review, I asked the question, and never really received a reply, "Who is in charge and who makes the decisions?" While their hardware was adequate to the tasks (including bi-coastal data centers for redundancy) I left feeling that when a major disaster hit, their response would be slowed and hampered because no one was in a position to make decisions or even to know what decisions to make.

So great, you've found and removed any dependencies you can find. You've determined who will be making the call, and determined who will be in charge once the call is made.

You're all set. Right?

Nope. You didn't really think it would be that easy.

Let's take a driving example. You probably recall being told if you start to slide or skid in a car, to look into the direction you want the car to go and steer in that direction. So, there's your DR plan for a skid in your car. All set? Of course you know the answer by now is, no.

Have you actually ever tried this? Have you ever gone out to a large, empty parking lot and tried to skid your car and recover?[1] If not, how do you know you'll succeed when this happens to you for real?

If you've done so in your old car, how do you know your new car will handle the same way? Or even if you have done it in your current car, how do you know you can still do it?

In vertical caving,[2] there are a number of skills cavers should be proficient at. One of these is known as a "change-over." During a change-over, a caver will transition from descending a rope to ascending a rope, or from ascending a rope to descending a rope. A thread came up on the National Speleological Society Cavechat forum several years ago asking if anyone had actually had to do a change-over in a cave. The actual number was quite small, but I was

---

[1]Note that you may want to check local laws before doing so. I am not responsible for any tickets you may receive practicing such maneuvers.
[2]Cavers in most of the world use a technique to get in and out of vertical caves called Single Rope Technique.

among them. The situation was a moderately dangerous one, but knowing how to do it because I had literally practiced it hundreds of times meant that I did it without issue, despite the situation (a minor issue with the rope actually gradually getting worse as I was doing the change-over.) Will I say having practiced change-overs saved my life? No, but it did keep the stress levels way down and probably made things much safer and easier.

There is also a rescue technique called a *pick-off*. Essentially, if someone gets stuck on a rope, a second caver can ascend the rope and "pick-off" the first caver off from their rope and lower them to the ground. This is in theory a technique I and most cavers are familiar with. However, I hazard a guess that most North American cavers could not do this in an actual cave if they had to in an emergency. The problem with this technique is if you fail to do it successfully, you can end up stuck on the rope. And now you've made the problem twice as bad, and potentially fatal.[3]

On the other hand, I have worked with European cavers who, due to their training, are expected to know how to do pick-offs in an expert fashion. In Hungary, caving leaders are required to be able to perform pick-offs in a timely and competent manner. As a result, these cavers practice their pick-offs on a continual basis and have very little doubt in their ability to perform them in an actual emergency.

In one case, a European caver I worked with probably barely massed 45kg and yet was able to consistently and cleanly pick me and my 100kg of body mass and equipment off in under three minutes.

Practice really is important.

For practice however, I recommend breaking the response down into individual steps and guaranteeing competency on each one before integrating them all together.

In the pick-off example, it's critical a caver be comfortable moving up and down a rope. Then they should be comfortable passing a knot or other obstructions. Once they are comfortable with this, they can start to practice a pick-off. Even then, I'd start outside in nice weather. Then perhaps I'd practice outside at night, when it's closer to the light conditions in a cave. In the end, you want to make your practice as close to the real thing as is safe and practical.

And, in all cases, I'd have a ladder available or a method of lowering the cavers if they get stuck while practicing. No one should be harmed or die during practice.

---

[3]I'm aware of at least once incident with two very inexperienced and ill-equipped cavers who died on rope as a result of a failed attempt at a pick-off.

This last one is an important detail. For any of your practices, you must have a backup plan. What if the practice goes sideways? What if your cavers get stuck on rope? What if your email failover practice fails and no email is being sent or received? Don't start your DR practice until you have these details nailed down. In a sense, have a DR plan for your DR plan. And we'll revisit this.

You should approach your DR plan the same way. Your ultimate DR plan may involve relocating all employees to a temporary office location and failing over to remote data center. Don't just wake up one morning and say, "OK, let's do a DR failover." Build up to it. Start simple. Perhaps first it will be, "OK, we'll see what's involved in moving our DNS Servers to our backup servers."

Then you might practice moving over your email to your backup provider. Then you may practice moving over your DNS and email.

That said, the reality is, you do have limited time and resources. You're not the only ones. In the 1960s, the United States embarked upon Kennedy's goal of landing a man on the moon. While it seemed like money was unlimited, it actually peaked in 1966 at $2.9 billion.[4] This meant that NASA had to make decisions. Originally, the goal and plan had been to test each stage of the Saturn V one at a time; that is, start with just a first stage (S-IC), fly that until all the kinks were worked out, then fly it with a S-IVB on top, fly that until the kinks were worked out, and so forth.

However, two issues were coming into play: time and money. The goal was to land a man on the moon (and return safely, an important detail) before the decade was out and to do so in a budget that was being increasingly scrutinized as the Vietnam War was building up. In 1963, there was tension between Wernher von Braun's team who favored an incremental approach and George Mueller, head of the NASA Office of Manned Space Flight who favored all-up testing (i.e., flying an entire Saturn V all at once and gathering as much data as could be gathered in that flight.) By 1964, Mueller's decision won the day.[5]

You may need to make similar decisions. At some point, you may not have the time and budget to test every individual step.

In addition, there's some testing that you probably just can't do. The number of these tests should be minimal but they may come up. For example, in the shuttle program, due to a variety of reasons there were some tests they couldn't fully do. For example, they could test a pad abort where they fired the engines on the orbiter itself (SSMEs) and they did a Flight Readiness Firing of each new orbiter and at other times.

---

[4]http://history.nasa.gov/SP-4029/Apollo_18-16_Apollo_Program_Budget_Appropriations.htm
[5]http://history.nasa.gov/SP-350/ch-3-4.html

They did a lot of practice aborts in the simulators where they tried to simulate as accurately as much as they could. That said, there was one abort mode that many astronauts had doubts about. It was known as a Return To Launch Site (RTLS) abort. In this mode, if an issue came up during the first two minutes of flight, the crew would prepare for an RTLS, but they could not initiate it until the SRBs were done firing. Then, basically they'd fly a specific flight profile where at high altitude they would turn the orbiter around toward Kennedy Space Center, and then drop the external tank and glide to the Shuttle Landing Facility.[6] There were doubts however, due to aerodynamic forces involved and other issues, on how survivable this abort mode was.[7]

Some people had suggested that STS-1 with John Young and Robert Crippen practice such an abort. John Young is quoted as saying surviving such a maneuver as "Six miracles followed by an act of God."[8]

I related these two cases, the Saturn V and the Space Shuttle not because I have an interest in space and space travel (though that's true) but because it illustrates that even when you have a huge budget and some of the best people working on your projects, you still have to make a final commitment and do as full a test as is safe and practical.

Back though to a point made a few pages previously. What happens if your test *does* go sideways? Be prepared. Even though John Young didn't want to fly the RTLS as a planned procedure, he would have had it been required. (And in fact, ironically after post-flight information came to light about damage to the body flap during lift off, Young said he would have flown an abort and ditched the orbiter had he known the extent of the damage).

As such, the Shuttle Landing Facility (as NASA called it, we'd call it a runway) was set up for a possible RTLS. The flight controllers were prepared for such an event and Young and Crippen had practiced it in the simulator.

When I teach SRT skills to beginner cavers, I make sure to provide a way to safely get them off the rope if things go wrong.

So, make sure your DR test has its own mini-DR plan. By the way, as you set up your mini-DR plan, this will help you discover other potential flaws in your actual DR plan.

So now, you're finally ready right? You've found and eliminated any dependencies you can find. You've determined who is in charge and can call for the DR plan to be put into action. You've done your testing. You're all set! Right?

---

[6]http://spaceflight.nasa.gov/shuttle/reference/shutref/sts/aborts/rtls.html
[7]http://www.nasa.gov/centers/johnson/pdf/383441main_contingency_aborts_21007_31007.pdf Chapter 1.4 .1
[8]*Into the Black: The Extraordinary Untold Story of the First Flight of the Space Shuttle Columbia and the Astronauts Who Flew Her* Rowland White page 203

Nope.

What about fail-back or as some call it, return to normal operations. You need to determine before your DR plan is initiated if this is feasible or even a requirement.

A very simple example is a *failover cluster*. If you have Windows Clustering set up and you practice a failover to make sure it works, you may determine there is no need to fail back. Either node should work as well as the other. Why have a second potentially disruptive event? During an actual DR event or during a DR test it may not be a requirement to failback to the original node.

At the other end of the spectrum, your DR plan may involve failing over to a remote data center. Once normal operations are restored or the DR test is over, you need to determine how to failback to the original office location. Or, you may need to determine a plan to failback to a new office location.

For example, if your office is consumed in a fire, your ability to fail back to the original location is nil. However, your requirement to fail over to a new, replacement office is probably very high.

OK, now you have your dependencies eliminated, your chain of command is clear, you've practiced your plan until you feel comfortable executing, you have your mini-DR plans for your DR plan, and you've got a failback plan.

Now are you ready?

Let me end simply by saying, "probably," but let's recall the quote at the start of this chapter: "No battle plan survives contact with the enemy." Despite all of this, in reality, nothing will go as you planned. NASA had never practiced the explosion of an O2 tank in the service module of the Apollo spacecraft during the outbound journey to the moon. Yet, because they had practiced so many other failure modes and could react to problems as they came up, they were able to save *Apollo 13*. So your actual disaster will probably not be exactly what you've prepared for, but you should be in a better position to react than if you had no plan.

Real-World Example: Ellison's Cave Rescue

Ellison's Cave in Georgia contains two of the deepest single drops in a cave in North America: Fantastic at 586 feet and Incredible at 440 feet. It is possible to do a through trip from two different entrances that require one to descend one of these and ascend the other. On May 26, 2013, a group of cavers entered Ellison's from the Incredible side of the cave and descended to the bottom of Incredible Pit. While travelling through the cave to the bottom of the previously rigged Fantastic Pit one of the cavers fell approximately 40 feet, severely injuring himself in the process. One of his companions completed the journey to Fantastic, ascended, exited the cave, and went for help.

Local authorizes responded as quickly as they could. Cave rescues in general tend to be complicated by factors such as access. Generally access to the entrance used for Fantastic is a one-mile uphill hike. For rescues, however, the plan involves the use of 4WD vehicles and old logging roads. A note in the plan suggests winching may be necessary. You can imagine how much more complicated this might be in rainy and muddy conditions.

In addition, once rescuers are at the entrance, this doesn't guarantee they know where the patient is or how to get to the patient. Ellison's has 12 miles of passage. Sending a rescue team to the wrong part of the cave can delay a rescue considerably.

It would be impossible to have a plan that includes detailed rescue instructions for each part of the cave. As a result, the Incident Commander (IC) has to have a good understanding of the cave and of the capabilities of the people available.

At the time of this rescue, the plans included how to gain access to the entrance for Fantastic and an idea of what equipment was required. However, there was no actual plan for rigging the 586-foot drop to raise a patient.

To carry out this rescue, several different objectives had to be accomplished:

- Communications had to be established as deep into the cave as possible. This allows the IC to make decisions in a timelier manner. This should be kept in mind for any incident you're involved with. Without communications, your response will be greatly slowed and you may make less than ideal decisions based on incomplete or outdated information.

- A medical team had to be dispatched to the patient in order to stabilize the patient for transport. You most likely won't have to deal with a medical issue in your incident, but replace this team with say with your server team, who is responsible for server installs. They will need the hardware and resources to rebuild a server.

- Rigging teams had to be used to rig the minimum of three drops between the patient and the outside world. Rigging for rescue is different from normal cave rigging because of the greater loads put on the systems and the fact that generally the patient cannot assist in raising or lowering themselves. This means the use of more advanced systems, such as systems employing mechanical advantage (i.e., pulleys set up to turn a system into a 2:1 or 3:1 or higher haul system) or perhaps what is known as a *counter-balance system*. In addition, belay lines need to be set up and places for crews to operate these systems are required. If a drop is tall enough (such as the 586-foot drop here) communications is critical. In your IT incident, this might be the network team that is providing a backbone for your other teams to plug into in order to get systems back up and running.

- Evacuation teams needed to be established. These folks are moving the patient, both below and above ground. They tend to be your stronger team members who may not necessarily have the technical training required for the other teams, but they are just as important. In IT terms, these may be the folks unboxing all the new computers, setting them on desks, and plugging in cables so that the OS and apps can be installed. The make-up of these teams may vary over time as people become available or have to leave for other duties. This is one area where you probably do *not* want to have a strict set of guidelines on who can perform these operations.

- A landing zone had to be established for the final evacuation. This also requires specialized people, but not necessarily for very long.

- In addition, there were details such as ordering the canteen truck, ordering four porta johns, and the like that needed to occur.

In all, there were 106 people onsite, 47 in the cave, and 24 people at the bottom of Fantastic. While many were members of the local Walker County Fire Rescue Cave and Cliff team and other local agencies, some where local cavers who were called because of their expertise. All cavers on scene had had training by the NCRC (National Cave Rescue Commission) and as such had at least a common baseline of experience. Many had more advanced training such as advanced medical training that allowed the introduction of IV fluids.

The initial estimate from the IC was 24 hours. It in fact took 26 hours to evacuate the patient and another six hours to demobilize the rescuers.

So, while the initial estimate was very close, the reality differed a bit.[9]

---

[9]Most of the above is based on discussions and emails with Allen Padget, former Georgia DEC Ranger and Incident Commander for this rescue.

Analysis

Most caves that are frequently visited and that have a higher than normal chance of rescue, such as Ellison's, tend to have written "pre-plans." In smaller caves, these plans can be fairly specific and detailed.

In the Weybridge rescue mentioned in the first chapter, the pre-plan explained exactly how much rock needed to be removed from a particular pinch-point in order to get a litter through. When an actual rescue came, this was used to guide the rescuers in rock removal and worked very well. However, a passage beyond that relied on a technique to move the litter that did not work. We had to improvise.

In other cases, the cave may be too complex or the number of dangers may be too high to create very specific plans. For example, had the accident detailed earlier happened at what is known as the *warm-up drop*, it's quite possible that the initial party could have gotten the patient to the top of the drop before any rescuers had shown up and the entire rescue taken less than four hours. But, much of the initial response and actions by the IC would have been similar (get a team to the entrance, establish communications to the patient, render appropriate medical care with the resources available, etc.)

Ellison's is such a large and complex cave, that attempting to detail a rescue plan for every possible scenario would be impractical and a waste of time. Making sure however that the people available have a general working knowledge and that details of a plan can be created on the fly is critical to a successful plan.

In a cave rescue, for example, you could learn that certain cavers who you want to use aren't available. Or worse, they're the ones requiring rescue! Or you may find that certain equipment can't make it to the location you want. This is going to be very true for any large scale IT incident. You might have a plan for replacing your office servers in the event of the loss of your building. But, then you discover the loss of your building is due to historic flooding and all roads are closed for a week so no delivery trucks can bring the replacement equipment to your office.

When creating your plan, don't confuse the goal or objectives with the plan to get there.

In Ellison's (as with any cave rescue) the objective was to get the patient to the hospital as quickly as possible and in as good or better shape than he was found.

Within that there were specific subgoals or objectives: establish communications, rig the drops, and so forth. Although some of them had written pre-plans (such as how to get people to the entrance), others didn't. And even when there were written plans they had to be adapted to the actual problems at hand.

According to the IC, Allen Padget, "The thing that really worked here was the fact that *all* resources utilized had been trained by the NCRC and understood the procedures/language of cave rescue."

It's also worth the reminder of a point I made in the previous chapters. Most incidents start small. While the seriousness of the incident in this case (both the injury itself and where in the cave it occurred) meant this was a major incident from the start, the response started out small. Not all 106 people appeared on-site at once. Not all parts of the plan were put into place all at once. As more people showed up, the Incident Commander and the various chiefs could start to build additional teams to solve individual parts of the incident as required. For example once there were an adequate number of people with rigging experience, the rigging problems could be addressed. Once the proper medical people were available, they could be assigned as required.

Even though this was a massive incident (as far as cave rescues go) it started small and the individual parts of the overall incident could each be addressed as relatively small problems. This is one reason I emphasize training and practicing for your disaster plan and using things like ICS; it gives you a common set of procedures and languages and make your response faster and better. But be prepared for things to change the minute your incident occurs.

Why Test?

Any parent who has school age children knows the reality of testing. And no, I don't mean the academic tests. Rather I mean the fact that their children will participate in fire drills while at school. And, in an unfortunate nod to today's world, most likely also participate in lock-down drills.

When many of us (or our parents) were in school, we participated in duck-and-cover drills.

The point of all this is two-fold: the first is to create an ingrained response to a specific disaster. The second is to ensure that the plan works.

For example, a component of a lock-down drill frequently includes the school principal or other administrator going from door to door to make sure that they are properly locked. If they're not, steps are taken to make sure that they're locked the next time.

For young children especially, it's critical to create an ingrained response. When they hear that it is a lock down, you want them to react promptly with little direction and discussion with the teacher. Time is of the essence.

As we get older, our "tests" may change, but testing and practice is still important. In the previous chapter, we discussed testing and when it may be practical and when it might not be. This chapter hopes to expand on that a bit more.

Let's discuss ingrained responses first. Early in the days when the Web was first getting popular, I was at a web-based company running an early version of SQL Server (6.0 at the time I believe). We used it heavily and apparently we were tripping over a bug. It wouldn't happen frequently, but when it did, our site would go down, which clearly wasn't acceptable to our customers.

© Greg D. Moore 2016

G. D. Moore, *IT Disaster Response*, DOI 10.1007/978-1-4842-2184-6_11

While the company worked hard on identifying the bug and a way to avoid it, my team and I had to actually deal with it. The response was fairly simple: restart the SQL Server Service.

For some reason lost to time, we couldn't easily automate this, but we did develop a way to detect when the problem occurred. A page was sent to the IT team. Then the person on duty would log in, restart the SQL Server Service, and it was good to go.

Within a few weeks, we had this down to under a 30-second response time. It was a purely rote reaction to a problem.

Now, many of your IT incidents aren't going to be nearly as clear-cut or have such a rote response, but that doesn't mean you can't practice them.

I mentioned change-overs for cavers. One reason why I practice them so much and encourage others is to develop the rote memorization and muscle memory. I'm not necessarily trying to set speed records (OK, I've been known to compete with a few others) but to make sure that I don't have to think too much about it. Why is this the case? Because when I am going to absolutely need to do it, is the time when I'm probably going to be least able to think clearly; that is, I'll probably be cold, wet, hungry, and tired from a day of caving but I have to perform a change-over. I don't want to have to spend any more time or brainpower on it than absolutely necessary.

On a similar note, airplane pilots also practice and test certain procedures on a regular basis so that they can respond quickly without thinking about the actual response.

Now consider something like a server failover. It would be ideal if they all happened during waking hours, with warning and no other distractions. But the reality is they often don't. This means that you may be woken from a deep slumber and called upon to execute a DR plan. Or you may be up for 24 hours executing a DR plan when some new issues come up.

When you do practice, start with a simple reproduction of the setup, perfect that, and then move up to more realistic setups. Eventually, you should feel comfortable practicing on a live system. I'll come back to this.

I noted in the last chapter that before I had to do a change-over in a cave in response to an actual problem with the rope, I had done change-overs hundreds of times beforehand. When I was teaching myself change-overs, I did so in my basement with a rope tied seven feet off the ground. I could climb up about one foot, change over, and come back down. It wasn't very realistic compared to a cave, but it was simple and I could practice it dozens of times. In fact, I greatly modified and simplified my technique, including eliminating my reliance on a piece of hardware. By removing this piece of hardware, I was able to perform my change-overs more reliably and quickly, and I had one fewer points of failure. I then graduated to doing it in a tree in the backyard where I was further off the ground and had more rope weight to contend with. I then did a caving trip where all I did was practice inside a cave.

I continued to refine and perfect my technique until I was able to practice it at about 450 feet off the bottom of the floor in Fantastic Pit in Ellison's Cave. Only after much practice did I feel comfortable doing it in such a location where rope weight and other factors were a serious issue.

I'll come back to this concept of building upon your practice in a bit.

The other reason to practice is because you'll quickly learn what will and won't work. When you do practice, throw in variables. OK, you can log into the VPN without any issues. But what if you're not using your standard desktop? Do you have the URL handy? Do you have access to passwords or emails that are required? If not, how can you get access?

Keep notes as you practice. You may find that your DR plan's return to normal operations requires you to be up and running in four hours. However, when you actually practice it, your testing shows it will take a minimum of eight hours.

Do you need to change your return to normal operations time or does your environment need to be upgraded? Perhaps it's taking eight hours because the tape robot is old and slow, and reading at one-fourth the speed that you expected. This would indicate that you need to replace your tape robot. Or perhaps the four-hour goal is simply unrealistic for that particular disaster and you need to convince management that a return to normal operations simply can't happen in less than eight hours.

Where possible, I recommend first setting up VMs to simulate your live environment. Make them as close to accurate as possible. Better yet, if you have the physical hardware to simulate your live environment, use that. Where possible, use actual copies of live data. Practice to make sure that the actual procedures work. Then, move on to the physical environment and practice there.

While not a DR plan per se, many companies require a change plan before doing major work. We discussed this idea in earlier chapters. In Chapter 5, I gave the example of planning the move of a data center using table-topping.

This was based on an actual experience. For our very first data center move, I used Visio to create a paper duplicate of every item in every rack that we were moving from and every rack we were moving to. I then spent hours "moving the data center" on paper. As I did so, I took notes. As I did this, I found many dependencies that I had not anticipated. I would then revise the plan and retest the move.

Only after the entire move had been fully documented and I had eliminated all potential dependencies were we ready to try it in a live situation. However, even before that could happen, we performed two other steps. I outlined timelines for how long I expected everything to take. In most cases, the times were such that if we were ahead of schedule, we could continue. But there were also fixed times in the plan. These were things like when a DNS change might have to be made and how long it would take to propagate. These were well noted.

In the second step, I went over the entire plan with my team so that each member knew their role and the roles of others.

Only then were we able to execute this in a live situation. And then of course it happened. Halfway through the execution, my manager walks in with a server on a dolly and says, "I brought up server X." I looked at our sheet and realized that he had failed to wait until the proper time and just brought our network down. He had failed to follow the plan because he had not practiced it with the rest of my team.

Fortunately, however, because we had tested everything else so well, we were able to quickly adapt and get things back online in under 15 minutes.

In Chapter 9, I mentioned the issues with a data center move at a different company. Some of the issues were because I did not table-top things like this. I failed to practice.

I mentioned when possible doing your practices in a live environment. This can be a hot topic when you bring it up among IT professionals. Many see it like the RTLS test of the space shuttle that I mentioned in the previous chapter: too dangerous to perform. Many see it more akin to performing a touch-and-go landing in an aircraft; something that should be able to be done without a second thought.

I'm firmly in the second camp. If anything, the inability to feel comfortable performing an RTLS abort in the space shuttle should give you pause for thought to exactly how robust the system is. If you don't feel your system is robust enough to perform a full-up failover test of major components, it may mean that your system is far more fragile than you care to admit. Now, admittedly, there are times when a system can't be made robust enough for a full-up test. In the early days of the space shuttle system, the computing power was limited and didn't permit analysis of the flight dynamics as the engineers wanted. Also, the overall knowledge of all the forces involved weren't known. For example, simply during launch, the acoustics were far worse than modeled and damaged a number of tiles and moved the body flap of the space shuttle further than expected.[1]

Even given the budget of NASA there were many unknowns due to factors such as limited computing power not under their control. However, for most of companies, we're not at that level of unknowns.

---

[1] http://www.jsc.nasa.gov/news/columbia/anomaly/STS1.pdf pages 5 and 27

At a previous employer, my network engineer and I wanted to (mostly at his behest) perform several network failover tests. The CTO and the VP of Development were opposed to this and outvoted me. They felt it was "too dangerous."

Now, my engineer and I were very confident that the test would be successful. But even more importantly, we felt that if something did go wrong, it was far better to learn in a controlled situation where we could do something. For example, if we had simulated a switch failure by powering off a switch (with someone physically at the switch to turn it back on) and found out that the network did not properly reconverge on the new switch due to an error in a configuration, we could simply power up the unpowered switch and be back at our starting point.

In that case, it would be far better to discover such an error with someone on-site to immediately correct the issue than one where the switch might really fail and no one was available to do anything about it.

So while we were confident we would succeed, we wanted to prove that we could.

Related to this sort of testing is often the question of when to perform such testing. This is partly based on the potential of risk and the magnitude of the risk. If my web-farm has N+2 redundancy on servers during peak load, I would have no problem doing a cold reboot of a server to perform a test during peak time. This proves that reboots will work and that our load-balancers can work. On the other hand, if our SQL Server is operating at maximum capacity during our peak time, and a failover takes five minutes and the company loses $1 million per minute of downtime, I'm probably going to be satisfied doing such as test late on a Saturday night at our slowest time.

From lessons learned, however, I probably would then go to my CFO and ask for a more robust SQL Server failover solution.

If the risk is low or the magnitude is low, I'll more likely want to do the test during business hours when more people are around to monitor and catch issues. If the risk is very high and/or the magnitude is very high, I am more likely to perform the test during off-hours and then build up to a test during office hours, if I can.

As I mentioned earlier, build upon your practice. If you think back to when you learned to drive, you most likely didn't immediately hop in the car and drive across the country. If you started in a stick-shift, you probably tried just moving the gear-shift back and forth until you got a feel for how it felt to go from first to second to third and back again.

Then you probably started on a deserted road and drove at slow speeds, shifting just a bit until you felt comfortable with shifting. Then you perhaps tried a busier road, or dealt with stopping at lights and handling intersections. Once you felt comfortable, you may have moved onto highway driving and driving at night.

In each case, you mastered a basic skill before moving onto a more complex one. This is very similar to how I learned and now teach single-rope technique skills for caving.

Similarly, this is how I recommend handling your DR plans. Start with something basic. Can you restore a SQL Server database? The first few times you'll probably have to check the syntax. And, if you're anything like many I've spoken to, you'll leave off the WITH NORECOVERY flag. For those not familiar with SQL Server, ironically, despite the name, if you leave *off* this flag, it makes it impossible to restore additional files to the database. So the first time you leave it off, you'll suddenly find yourself unable to continue with recovering the database and have to start over.

Once you get to the point where you can recover the database without having to look up the syntax and make a simple mistake like the one I described, practice the steps to make sure your users have access to the database. Don't worry about having the application itself access the database; just focus on getting to the point where users can access the database directly. Then work on the application.

While I fully recommend a checklist for all of this (per the discussion in Chapter 5), a checklist is not very useful if you have little practice doing the actual steps. And, of course, in a full disaster scenario, your documentation may be lost or unavailable, so it helps to have an idea of what is required.

Think of it using the central-line example from Chapter 5. The addition of a checklist helped doctors reduce their infection rate from 11% to 0%. But, the checklists didn't replace the doctor's knowledge of how to do a central line—that is, a checklist didn't suddenly make it possible for an untrained person to insert a central line, but a trained person could still do a central line without a checklist.

Real-World Example: Cluster Failover Failure

One of the companies I worked for acquired another company that had a product based on a Linux and MySQL platform. Despite my lack of direct experience with those platforms, I was asked to help monitor a move to a new MySQL Cluster setup.

About a week before the new company was ready to go live, I scheduled some testing. Part of the test involved simply shutting down one node of the cluster and making sure that the second node took over the MySQL processing.

We performed the shutdown and the second node took over without issues. However, after five to ten minutes, the initial node was still not back up. We tried several things, including remotely cycling the power, but nothing would bring it back. This was obviously not the desired outcome.

However, my reason for the test had been vindicated. Despite being assured that everything was set up correctly, something wasn't right. Had this happened while in production, we could have had a potentially serious problem.

Analysis

We called the vendor that installed the cluster and they assured us over and over again that the problem could not be in their setup and that they had tested the exact setup we were testing.

We finally had to send someone to the data center in order to attach a terminal to the node and see what was or wasn't happening.

When the engineer got there, the problem was obvious but perplexing. The node that wasn't fully up was sitting at a prompt trying to mount a share off of an unknown computer. At first we thought perhaps something had been hacked. Then the engineer recognized the name of the unknown computer. It was the name of the laptop the consulting company used when setting up the nodes of our cluster.

He was able to get past that and remove the mount command and reboot the node. The node came up without incident. We then proceeded to retest the cluster failover in each direction. This time it operated without fail.

We called the vendor and asked them about the mount command. As we expected, they used the laptop to load drivers and other software during the initial configuration of the nodes. The mount was supposed to be removed after the entire setup was complete. It obviously wasn't.

And yes, the vendor had performed a reboot test similar to ours, but while their laptop was still plugged into the network. So for them, the testing was a success.

Finding this sort of issue is exactly why I argue for making testing as accurate and realistic as possible. Had this happened in production, it's quite possible the failover might have failed, or the cause for the failover could have also caused the second box to shortly fail and we'd have had no bootable nodes.

I will add that when we reached the point in our testing where the original node failed to come up, we did not continue with the test. The next steps were to then reboot the second node to show that the system would fail back. Obviously, in this case, there was nothing to fail back to, so rebooting the second node would only have made things worse.

That said, once the problem with the setup was fixed, we performed the originally planned test to confirm that all would work as expected. This time it did.

Swiss Cheese

"It seems that perfection is attained not when there is nothing more to add, but when there is nothing more to remove."

—Antoine de Saint Exupéry in *Terre des hommes* (1939)

No, I'm not saying I have nothing more to add or that this book is perfect. But, as the perfect disaster is the one that never happens, we'll talk a bit about that in this chapter.

I haven't touched upon it, but in accident theory, there's a model known as the "Swiss cheese model."[1] The basic idea is that for an accident to occur, several pieces of "cheese" have to line up so that you can see through all the holes. If one piece of cheese is moved, the holes no longer line up and no accident will occur. An example might be the incident I described in Chapter 9, where we had a SAN failure and NAS failure, and a few failures not described in that analysis. Had the SAN not failed, the disaster would have been minimal. Had the NAS not failed, the disaster would have been hardly worth noting. Change a single parameter slightly and you can greatly change the outcome.

This is critical because it means that if we can see into the future, we can sometimes shift a piece of "cheese" to where we want it to be rather than allow randomness to let it fall where it may. Or better, we can make the "cheese" holes smaller or even eliminate them altogether.

Specifically, this comes down to disaster prevention and mitigation.

---

[1] https://en.wikipedia.org/wiki/Swiss_cheese_model for a more detailed introduction with links to better sources.

© Greg D. Moore 2016
G. D. Moore, *IT Disaster Response*, DOI 10.1007/978-1-4842-2184-6_12

Disaster Mitigation

First, let's make the cheese holes smaller. This means the disaster in scope is smaller: disaster mitigation.

Disaster mitigation can take many forms. In an IT world, it can be RAID disks. We know that disks will fail. So, if we use a form of RAID, such as 1 or 5, we can mitigate any potential disaster. We don't completely eliminate it, but we do reduce the impact. For example, with RAID 5, if a disk fails, we lose some performance until the disk is replaced and the parity data is rebuilt. But we don't completely lose our data. We've mitigated the disaster a bit.

Most of what we focus on is disaster mitigation. We can never completely eliminate the potential for hardware failure in the IT business. At best, we can mitigate the effects. At worst, though, we can make them worse.

What's even better than making the cheese holes smaller is eliminating them altogether: disaster prevention.

Disaster Prevention

Disaster prevention is a trickier business. For the purposes of this chapter, I want to give it a more precise definition. Disaster prevention is taking steps to ensure that a particular form of a disaster can never occur.

To give you an example, the *SS United States* was a luxury passenger liner built in 1952. Although designed as a passenger liner, it was also designed for potential use as a troop ship in the time of war. Fire was one of the potential disasters that the builders wanted to eliminate. As a result, almost everything on board was designed to be non-flammable. Even the grand piano was built from a fire-resistant form of wood.[2] This eliminated an entire class of disaster.

Eliminating disasters can actually be harder than you think. In many cases, people approach the elimination by adding more pieces of hardware, or more infrastructure, or more procedures to be followed. What they miss is that this can introduce entirely new places for an incident to occur. Let me give two examples.

In the first case, consider a typical private airplane. If you ask most non-pilots which is safer, a single-engine airplane or a twin-engine airplane, they'll naturally reply that the twin-engine aircraft is safer because it has two engines, so if one fails, you've still got a second engine. This is a very logical assumption to make. It can also be very wrong, for several reasons. For one, the loss of one engine on a twin engine plane can result in loss of 80% of power. This may not be enough to keep the plane in the air.[3]

[2]https://en.wikipedia.org/wiki/SS_United_States
[3]https://www.aopa.org/training-and-safety/pic-archive/flight-training-ratings-and-proficiency/single-vs-twin

In addition, with only one engine, directional control is severely hampered and stability is greatly impacted.[4]

Finally, if you think about it, if engines have a certain MTBF (mean time between failures), two engines are more likely to fail in the same amount of time as one. This is similar to how RAID works. In fact, twin-engine planes are in many ways more like RAID 0 than RAID 1!

Does this mean that twin-engine planes are automatically less safe than single-engine planes? No. It simply means you've potentially introduced failure modes and increased the chance of a failure. On the other hand, in an emergency, you've potentially given yourself more options if you have the proper training and know what to do.

Another example is when training a caver for a long rappel into a pit. Rappelling can be one of the more dangerous activities that cavers do on a rope because if they start to accelerate too quickly, they may overcome their own ability or the ability of their equipment to stop them before they suffer acute rock poisoning at the bottom of the pit; that is, they hit the bottom at a high speed and are severely injured or die.

There are several methods that can be used to mitigate this potential disaster. Some folks suggest the use of a separate belay line from the top. This can eliminate the problem of a rappeller going too fast. But, it now introduces a new potential disaster. For various reasons, the rappeller may start to rotate around this rappel line. If they have a belay line on them, this can start to twist around their main line and become tangled. This can cause them to be stuck on the rope, with the inability to ascend or descend.

An alternative is to perform what's known as a fireman's belay at the bottom, which is essentially a person putting tension (sometimes to the point of hanging on it) on the main line. This can cause the rappeller to stop. However, it now puts a person at the bottom of the pit into a potential fall zone where any rocks or debris knocked off by the rappeller can potentially hit them.

So, while either solution may eliminate one potential disaster, there is the potential to introduce other disasters that could have equally bad outcomes.

For a far more detailed look at this concept, I highly recommend the book *Normal Accidents* by Charles Perrow (Princeton University Press, 1999).

Now, as I mentioned, in IT, we can't fully eliminate all hardware or software disasters. If we did, we'd have no infrastructure left. But we can take steps to reduce some and eliminate others.

---

[4]http://www.multiengineairplane.com/flying-on-one-engine/

Early in my career, thin-wire Ethernet (10Base2) was the de facto method of networking computers. But it had a horrible failure mode. If the cable broke in any location, none of the computers on that segment could talk to the servers. One reason that 10Base-T replaced 10Base2 was because by designing a network into a physical star pattern (as opposed to the physical ring pattern of a 10Base2 network), a single cable break only impacted only the computer that it was attached to. This and differences in the cabling design helped to eliminate one class of disaster (entire segments of the network going offline) and reduce other forms of disasters (cable breaks due to a BNC adapter coming loose, etc.).

When you go through your infrastructure, think about how you can eliminate or reduce disasters. I used to travel with a laptop a lot. By ensuring that I had multiple chargers (one at the office, one at the data center, and one in my bag), I basically eliminated the chance of getting to the data center, two hours from the main office, and discovering that I had no way of keeping my laptop running. By standardizing to one laptop brand in the office, if someone left their charger at home, we were more likely to be able to loan one for the day.

Where else can you do the same? Your data center can standardize to just two classes of hardware for the server, even if it means for certain servers you're deploying something a bit beefier than you might otherwise need. This gives you flexibility that if a more important server has failed, you can swap in the other server and perhaps off-load its functionality to another server or eliminate it for the time being.

You might have heard about standardizing things. This is what you're doing. You're standardizing to mitigate the impact of a disaster. Ideally, you're also eliminating the potential disaster of not having easy access to replacement parts.

In terms of procedures and protocols, it's also important to eliminate disasters where you can, and mitigate them where you can.

Another way to avoid a disaster is to see it coming. Now, if you haven't completely fallen asleep or forgotten the first chapter, you'll remember that I defined a disaster as "an unplanned interruption in business that has an adverse impact on finances or other resources." If that's true, how can you see one coming?

Consider it more of a prediction, and not an absolute certainty. Going into New Year's Eve 1999, many people predicted all sorts of disasters caused by the Y2K problem. At my employer, we prepared for it and had a fully operational command center and more. And yet, so little happened. Why? Because people saw the potential and worked to avert as much of it as they could.

The reality is the Y2K problem first reared its head long before it came to popular attention. Even in the late 1960s and early 1970s, some banks became aware of it as they tried to handle 30-year mortgages. As we got closer to the year 2000, more and more potential points of failure were found and mediated. Despite that, there were still isolated incidents that showed up on New Year's Day 2000. But overall, the total number was relatively small and many predicted disasters were avoided because of the precautions taken.

If only that was the last such example. If you've worked long enough with computers, you've probably heard of the Y2K38[5]. This is a clear example of an upcoming issue that may be an issue for many companies in the next couple of decades. Now is the time to start thinking about how to eliminate or mitigate the potential disasters from it in your company.

There are many other potential issues that are known out there that you should be aware of.

But what about those issues that are internal to your organization? When you do have a large disaster, a post-mortem is a critical piece to perform. I won't go into the details of how to conduct one here, but I will give a software-related example.

In the early days of the space shuttle program, testing was being done to the shuttle arm when it suddenly stopped working. The issue was traced to a bug in the code: if the arm rotated 360 degrees, it thought it had gone past 360 degrees, and the software didn't know what to do.

Rather than fix that bug, clap each other on the back, and go home, the programmers dug through their code and found eight other places in the code where there was potential for the same bug to impact a particular piece of hardware.[6]

The Human Factor

One topic that I've skirted around is the human factor. In Chapters 6 and 7, I talked about people involved in disasters, how they react differently, and how to manage people during a disaster.

But here I want to make a very important point: people are often the single biggest factor in the *cause* of a disaster. Fortunately, they can also be the single biggest factor in recovering from a disaster.

On June 1st, 2009, Air France Flight 447 crashed into the Atlantic Ocean. The entirety of events is too long and complex to delve into here. (If you want to read the final report, the URL to it is footnoted at the bottom of the page.[7])

---

[5]https://en.wikipedia.org/wiki/Year_2038_problem
[6]https://www.fastcompany.com/28121/they-write-right-stuff
[7]https://www.bea.aero/docspa/2009/f-cp090601.en/pdf/f-cp090601.en.pdf

The disaster involved a number of factors that include programming decisions made years prior, as well as design decisions in how the cockpit was laid out and how equipment would respond to human input. So, at the risk of incurring the ire of pilots and experts, I will greatly simplify the story of what happened.

It appears that while flying at altitude, the pitot tubes, which tell the airspeed of the aircraft, iced over, and thus gave incorrect data to the pilot. It appears that the pilot responded to the warnings in a manner inconsistent with the actual state of the aircraft. As a result, he apparently put the plane into a stall, which ultimately resulted in it impacting with the ocean and killing all aboard.[8]

While it's easy to point the finger at a mechanical failure, the pitot tubes icing over, or at design flaws, ultimately it was pilot error that doomed the aircraft. This was all the pieces of cheese coming together at once, but the one thing that could be changed, the human reaction, wasn't. The pitot tube issue and the design issues obviously couldn't be changed. It was up to the pilot to make the correct decision and it appears that he did not. In addition, it appears that failure to properly use CRM led to confusion as to what information was transmitted from the Captain, who was on a rest break, to the Pilot Flying and the Pilot Not Flying. This most likely led to confusion as to which pilot was physically in control of the aircraft and which pilot thought they were actually in command. Essentially, they did not know who was flying the aircraft! [9]

This is far from the only case of an aircraft crashing because of improper crew response.[10]

If you stop to think about it, very rarely do you hear about a major airline experiencing a crash strictly due to mechanical failure. For the most part, mechanical failures due to design issues (as opposed to improper maintenance or other factors) have been engineered out of the system. A review of accidents over the last decade or so will show that most are due to pilot error. However, on the flip side, many of the more spectacular recoveries are also due to pilot training. US Airways Flight 1549, the Miracle on the Hudson, is a textbook example of pilots using their training and skills to respond to a rapidly deteriorating situation in such a way that resulted in zero loss of life. I also discussed United Airlines Flight 232. Unlike Flight 1549, which was the result of an external event, the bird strike, UA Flight 232 was the direct result of an internal mechanical failure. By all accounts, the plane was deemed unflyable. Yet with effort, the flight crew was able to execute a landing that saved the lives of 185 people. So although the human factor is often the direct cause of a disaster, the human factor can also be a major factor in response to a disaster.

---

[8]Ibid page 17
[9]Ibid page 185
[10]Ibid page 161

In IT terms, the closest example I can think of is that through the use of things like RAID controllers, we've pretty much eliminated disk failure in certain circumstances, yet we still hear of the repair person coming in and pulling the wrong disk. Or we hear about an IT person shutting down the wrong server. This is the final piece of Swiss cheese coming into place at the wrong time. Work to eliminate that mode of failure if you can, but also ultimately realize that the same people that might cause some failures are the only ones that can solve many others.

Real-World Example: Unlocked Door

Several years ago, I sat in during a meeting of my alma mater's Outdoor Club. During executive session, the students brought up an issue involving access to the club's indoor climbing wall.

To access the wall, you had to give your student ID to the student working in the equipment room, who in turn gave you the key to lock and unlock the door to the climbing wall gym. Upon leaving, the student was supposed to lock the door and return the key to get their student ID back. It was each student's job to make sure that the door was locked. In theory, it was the student worker's job to confirm that the door was locked. Failure to do so was a risk-related issue, because it meant someone without proper training and equipment could go into the climbing gym, climb the wall, and potentially be injured.

Since my alma mater is an engineering school (Rensselaer Polytechnic Institute), I listened as possible solutions to the issue were discussed. At first, who had failed to lock the door was the focus. Finally, one of the students pointed out that it wasn't worth dwelling on—they had to focus on preventing an unlocked door in the future.

So the students discussed several ideas. One that stood out was installing a webcam to observe the door so that the student worker could monitor it. Everyone felt that this was a good solution because it added redundancy and the status of the door could be checked at any time.

Analysis

As far as I know, the solution proposed was not the one adopted. Why? Because, as I pointed out to everyone at the time, it was actually not that great of a solution—for two reasons. The first was the most obvious. A webcam didn't actually ensure that the door was locked. It wouldn't change the root cause—someone failing to lock the door.

The second reason was more subtle. Webcam monitoring added another task to someone who was already tasked with enough jobs. The student worker (in addition to the student who had signed out the key in the first place) had failed to notice the unlocked door, despite it being an assigned task. I pointed out that assigning yet another task on top of an existing task load made it more prone to failure.

I suggested instead that they request that the building maintenance people replace the door with a self-locking door; that is, the sort of door that locks behind you. This wouldn't prevent folks inside the climbing gym from leaving, and since no rules prevented them from propping the door open while folks were in the room, it wouldn't keep people out unnecessarily. But, since it's a pretty ingrained habit to close a door if you're the last person to leave such a room (though apparently not to lock it) the last person would by default lock it without actually having to do anything more than what they normally did. In fact, a self-locking door eliminated a step in the procedure and eliminated the failure of someone locking it. (Now, admittedly, it did introduce new failures— the self-locking mechanism not working or the door not closing all the way. But those were deemed acceptably low risks.)

The moral of the situation is this: don't rely on adding infrastructure to make things more robust. Perfection (or something close to it) may be reached when we remove some of the infrastructure, not add more to it.

Epilogue

"All good things must come to an end."

—Chaucer

Part of the motivation for writing this particular book came out of offering my local SQL Server User Group an option on one of two talks. They could hear a talk by me on Microsoft's Entity Framework and the drawbacks from a DBA's point of view, or a talk on why planes crash and what IT can learn from it. It wasn't very on-topic for a SQL Server User Group, but I was curious to see if I'd get any takers. Apparently, the DBAs were more interested in plane crashes than they were in learning about Entity Framework. This was actually a blessing in disguise since I had most of the slides for the plane crash presentation prepared. I still have yet to write up the slides for a talk on Entity Framework.

As I stated in Chapter 1, many books on IT disasters discuss how to make sure that you have backups and redundant disks, and so forth. I didn't want to focus on that. While all of this is very important, at the end of the day, it's the human factor that can often make the difference between a success and a failure.

It's been said that there are two types of people: those who run away from the fire and those who run toward it. (It's also been said of two types of people: those who can count to 10 and those who don't understand binary. If you don't get that joke and still enjoyed this book, then I'm particularly pleased. If you did get the joke and still enjoyed the book, that's great too.)

© Greg D. Moore 2016
G. D. Moore, *IT Disaster Response*, DOI 10.1007/978-1-4842-2184-6_13

I've never been a firefighter or a police officer, so I can't say I've ever directly put myself in harm's way like they do. And I don't want to equate what we do when we handle an IT disaster with the dangers faced by those who routinely put their lives on the line. But that said, I do think it's generally true that there are those who see a disaster as a moment to shine and apply their knowledge and skills, and there are those who turn to others to lead them. I've always found myself in the former group. While I don't look forward to an IT disaster or a cave rescue, I do appreciate being able to put my skills and knowledge to work when they come up. Hopefully, you're like that too.

The quote at the start of this chapter refers both to the end of this book (I'd like to think it was good read and I hope you did to) and to the fact that every company faces a potential disaster every day. And if you're reading this book, you're probably the one that will be expected to put your skills and knowledge to the test.

During the *Apollo 13* flight, all the pieces of the "Swiss cheese" came together and created a potentially deadly disaster. A dropped oxygen tank that underwent extra testing, which was performed incorrectly due to the wrong specification being used, exploded in midflight. Had almost none of these issues occurred (the tank never being dropped, the test not being performed incorrectly, the cyro stir being performed when it was), the flight might have had a completely different outcome.

More recently, the passengers on US Airways Flight 1549 had no idea that their flight to Seattle, Washington, would end a scant six minutes later on the Hudson River. Many call this incident the Miracle on the Hudson, but when you look more closely, you realize that a lot of training and skills went into turning this event into a successful ditching instead of a deadly disaster.

In the Weybridge cave rescue that I mentioned earlier, the pre-plan did not turn out be fully workable in practice. But through the skills and knowledge of all the rescuers present, we were able to safely get the patient out of the cave.

In all of these cases, an important element was the human factor. Plans existed, but as mentioned earlier, none of the plans survived first contact with the actual disaster. However, the people involved adapted, often on the fly, and made the best decisions that they could.

However, the people involved didn't just muddle around, or worse, loose their cool when their original plans fell apart. They used many, if not all, of the components expressed in this book. Captain Sullenberger and First Officer Skiles used CRM to manage the incident within the cockpit and in their communications with air traffic controllers. The other rescuers and I were part of an Incident Command System in the Weybridge rescue. We communicated using the terms we had learned in training and we knew what skills and abilities we could rely on with each other.

During the Apollo program, the controllers at mission control and the astronauts spent thousands of hours in simulators, practicing almost everything they thought could go wrong. Despite never practicing the exact disaster of *Apollo 13*, their combined years of practice at solving the individual problems they faced (powering down the CSM, powering up the LM on a greatly reduced timeline, transferring the state vectors for navigation, performing burns without the aid of the on-board computer, and many more) were solved in an adequate fashion. Even the unexpected course deviation caused by the ice sublimator was handled as it cropped up.[1]

Over the years, I've amassed a collection of books on the topic of disasters and survival. I've also read numerous articles online and spoken with numerous people who work in situations where they respond to disasters or potential disasters that can have tragic consequences. I would say that makes me better educated than some, but there is always more to learn.

I'd like to list some of the authors whose books have influenced me.

Charles Perrow: Author of *Normal Accidents: Living with High-Risk Technologies* (Basic Books, 1984) and also *The Next Catastrophe: Reducing Our Vulnerabilities to Natural, Industrial, and Terrorist Disasters* (Princeton University Press, 2007).

These are a great pair of books that look at how the complexity of systems may inevitably lead to accidents, and how we can reduce or mitigate some of the issues, but never fully eliminate them and maintain the lifestyles that we have now. He also focuses on how we sometimes spend too much energy on certain classes of disasters without taking into account the probability of them. For example, right after 9-11, the US Department of Homeland Security/FEMA strongly focused on the next terrorist attack, while not focusing enough on natural disasters such as Hurricane Katrina.

Laurence Gonzales: Author of *Deep Survival* (W. W. Norton & Company, 2004), *Everyday Survival* (W.W. Norton & Company, 2008), and *Surviving Survival* (W.W. Norton & Company, 2013).

This set of books gets into the mind-set of people in the midst of disasters and how they successfully (or not so successfully) respond to them. The books illustrate how important the mind-set of the people involved can be.

James Lovell and Jeffrey Kruger: Author of *Lost Moon: The perilous Voyage of Apollo 13* (Houghton Mifflin, 1994).

This is a deeply personal and intimate look at what happened on *Apollo 13* with a great deal of detail. I also highly recommend the movie (based on the book) *Apollo 13*, directed by Ron Howard.

Andy Weir: Author of *The Martian* (Crown, 2014).

---

[1]Lost Moon - Page 351

While a completely fictional account, Mark Whatney and NASA exhibit some great problem solving and it also shows the limits on responding to a disaster due to limited communications, information, and resource. Whatney survives with a lot of skill and training and a bit of luck. The movie is also well worth watching.

Richard Feynman: Author of *Surely You're Joking Mr. Feynman* (W. W. Norton & Company, 1997) and *What Do You Care What Other People Think?* W. W. Norton & Company, 2001).

A genius in the field of theoretical physics, as well as a bit of a raconteur, Feynman approached problems often with a different approach than others which allowed him to gain an insight that others may have missed. Partly famous for his role in bringing to light the effect of the cold on the SRB O-Rings, he made a point of writing up his own thoughts on the poor risk analysis NASA had done on the Space Shuttle program. This write-up is included in the second of the two books listed above. An important point he made was that, "For a successful technology, reality must take precedence over public relations, for nature cannot be fooled." This needs to be applied to disaster responses and preparedness. Disasters will unfold as they are wont to do, spin and PR can't change that. You can claim that you can restore the ITB server in 30 minutes, but until you've tested it under the same conditions as you'd experience during a disaster, it's just a feel-good statement.

Atul Gawande: Author of *The Checklist Manifesto* (Metropolitan Books, 2009).

A fast read that gives far more insight into the history of checklists and how they can be used, and equally important, where they aren't effective.

Other Books and Resources

I also perused several NTSB reports and other documents in gathering some background for some of the chapters in this book.

I also have relied on my experience and training as a cave rescue instructor with the National Cave Rescue Commission and as a participant in several cave rescues when it comes to several of the incidents mentioned here.

I recommend that if you find this book interesting or useful, you should read any or all of the books listed in this chapter. I also suggest general reading on plane disasters (Wikipedia is a good place to start) and any of the various histories and biographies about the US space program. I also recommend reading what you can about the Russian (formerly Soviet) and Chinese space programs to get a better understanding of how each agency approaches risk.

Although I didn't cover it all in this book, I also suggest reading about the OODA loop. This refers to the process of Observe, Orient, Decide, Act. Although developed for combat situations, it has applications in decision-making processes during a disaster, especially one that is fast paced.

Finally, although I can't provide a specific title and I didn't use any for this book, I recommend reading up on how the US Navy handles operations in general, but specifically upon the deck of a carrier and in their nuclear submarine operations. After the failure of the *USS Thresher* (SSN-593), the Navy instituted SUBSAFE to ensure the safety of submarine operations. Since then, no submarine certified under the SUBSAFE program has been lost at sea.

The following are some other web sites to review:

- US Department of Homeland Security FEMA Emergency Management Institute - National Incident Management System https://training.fema.gov/nims/

- US Navy Flight Deck Awareness Basic Guide http://www.public.navy.mil/navsafecen/Documents/media/FDA/FDA-5thEd.pdf

- Safety during operations, occupational safety - MIT OpenCourseWare `https://ocw.mit.edu/courses/aeronautics-and-astronautics/16-863j-system-safety-spring-2011/lecture-notes/MIT16_863JS11_lec10.pdf`

When I set out to write this book, one of my goals was to show how disaster response can benefit from a multi-disciplinary approach. Hopefully, after reading this book and the suggested reading, you also can see the value of this approach.

In cave rescue, because every cave is different, the approach we take is to fill up the student's "toolbox" with skills and ideas that they can use as appropriate. For example, when rigging for a haul, we teach several different techniques. In the event of an actual rescue, the rescuer can choose the one that's appropriate based on the equipment and the personnel available. For example, for rigging Fantastic Pit in Ellison's Cave, the rescuers are prepared to do it one of multiple ways. What they choose depends on the particulars of the rescue.

Similarly, each chapter in this book should give you a tool or a set of tools to use as appropriate. You may not need to use any of the CRM lessons from Chapter 4 in one disaster, but in a different disaster, find that with multiple people involved, it's critical to set up clear communications and clarify who is in charge.

As seen in the suggested reading, there are even more tools that you can potentially add to your toolbox, such as the OODA loops, lessons from the SUBSAFE program, and more.

That all said, writing this book has been a fun and interesting experience. It was on my mind for actually over a decade, but the recent talk on plane crashes was the real impetus for writing it.

Maybe now that I'm done with this book I can go back and write that presentation on Entity Framework. Somehow I doubt it though. It still doesn't seem nearly as interesting a topic and there's a lot more interesting books on my shelf and articles online to read. And I think a lot more can be written on this subject.

Thanks for reading!

Appendix

This appendix contains a partially written sample checklist used before a data center move and test.

I used a partially written checklist to illustrate some of the thinking that goes into a checklist like this. It was a work in progress. Some questions had to be answered before the change/review plan (CRP) could be used. Some questions are designed to be answered the first time it is run, such as how long the initial SAN sync might take. While we can calculate bandwidth, until we test it, we don't know for sure. (In reality, I discovered that the specced performance numbers from the data center were woefully wrong and the initial sync took longer than planned.)

As discussed in Chapters 10 and 11, even the change plan discusses the disasters that might come up during testing.

What's not written yet is the rollback procedure. This needs to be written before the CRP can be executed.

Also obviously missing are the signatures of key people, which are needed for approval. I've had some CRPs that required the CEO to sign because despite the risk of a problem being very low, if a particular failure did occur, it would create major issues for the company. Since this was a test of a DR center and not actual production, a CEO's signature wasn't required here.

© Greg D. Moore 2016
G. D. Moore, *IT Disaster Response*, DOI 10.1007/978-1-4842-2184-6_14

Change Review Plan

Plan: Test DR plan in the new data center

Author: Greg D. Moore

Version: 0.8

Date: 2016-09-28

Goal

Develop and test a disaster plan in new data center before going live.

Reason

We will have a limited window to perform this test without impacting production operations. In order to have a useful and functional DR plan, it must be tested before it is required.

Note: After the failover plan has been tested at least once and changes have been documented, a determination should be made on whether it's necessary to test again. If so, update this CRP and then redo test.

Assuming the changes are minor or in the documentation only, then the documented failover plan should be tested in a real-world scenario with little warning and by the folks who will most likely be expected to carry out the failover.

In summary, this CRP is to confirm and improve the failover procedure. A separate actual test should be run if time permits.

Plan

Preliminary

Set up the following DNS:

- bostest.disastercorp.com point to web farm in the Boston, MA, data center

- austest.disastercorp.com point to web farm in the Austin, TX, data center

- prodtest.disastercorp.com initially point to web farm in the Austin, TX, data center 5min TTL

(Question: Can we use BGP to redirect prodtest.disastercorp.com between data centers and do this in real time?)

With existing data in various both data centers:

Megan, perform testing (part of an ongoing process, not necessary to do anything specific here.)

Decide on the size of the initial "sync" of data between PROD and DR.

Decide on the sync method (the two plans are outlined next).

Notes should be taken during the test, especially on the time required for each step.

Items to Review

`http://msdn.microsoft.com/en-us/library/ms151224(v=sql.90).`
`aspx`

SAN Sync

(Plan at least 24 hours for initial sync.)

1. Back up the database files on USBOSDB01CI2\ DRSQLDB01 (30 minutes?)

   Also back up install?

2. Put up a "down for maintenance" message.

3. Stop SQL Server on USBOSDB01CI2\DRSQLDB01. (1 minute)

4. Begin sync (initial estimate 300GB will take 22 hours or more). (22 hours)

5. Confirm that initial sync is complete. (1 minute)

6. Stop SQL Server USAUSDBCI2\PRDDB01. (1 minute)

7. Confirm that sync is up to date. (1 minute)

8. Start SQL Server USBOSDB01CI2\DRSQLDB01. (30 minutes)

   a. Since this has a different masterdb (the one from USAUSDBCI2) and it is configured for that server, how will this work? Do more research on this.

   b. Do we have to rename the server configure? Update internal DNS?

   c. How will jobs work? (The paths will all point to AUS!)

9. Confirm via SSMS that the databases on USBOSDB01CI2\ DRSQLDB01 are accessible. (1 minute)

10. Change prodtest.disastercorp.com to point to the Boston data center. (1 minute)

11. Build replication to USBOSDB19\DRRPT01 (1 hour)

    a. May need to remove replication to USAUS11DB51\ PRDRPT01.

    b. Build scripts for this!

12. Use bostest.disastercorp.com to confirm that the web farm can reach the database. (1 minute)

13. Use prodtest.disastercorp.com to confirm that the failover has worked and the data is accessible. (30 minutes)

14. Test backup jobs and other maintenance jobs. (3 hours)

15. Any other additional tests?

16. Reverse SAN replication back to AUS. (Is replication two-way or do we need 30 hours for this?) (30 hours – worst case)

17. Put up a "down for maintenance" message.

18. Confirm that initial sync BOS->AUS is complete.

19. Stop SQL Server USBOSDB01CI2\DRSQLDB01.

20. Confirm that sync BOS->AUS is up to date.

21. Start SQL Server USAUSDBCI2\PRDDB01.

    a. May have to rename the server again.

    b. May have to update DNS.

    c. Review jobs.

22. Confirm via SSMS that the databases on USAUSDBCI2\ PRDDB01 are accessible. (1minute)

23. Change prodtest.disastercorp.com to point to the AUS data center. (1 minute)

24. Build replication to USAUS11DB51\PRDRPT01. (1 hour)

    a. May need to remove replication to USBOSDB19\ DRRPT01.

    b. Build scripts for this!

25. Use AUStest.disastercorp.com to confirm that the web farm can reach the database. (1 minute)

26. Remove the "down for maintenance" message.

27. Use prodtest.disastercorp.com to confirm that the fail-back works and data is accessible. (30 minutes)

28. Test backup jobs and other maintenance jobs. (3 hours)

29. Reverse SAN replication back to AUS->BOS.

Log Shipping

We need to determine if we log ship with the "sync with backup" option. I suggest that we do not (since we're assuming failover of the data center).

Note: We should do this twice. Once as a scheduled log ship (where we know in advance the logs are properly shipped). The second time without logs properly shipped.

```
http://msdn.microsoft.com/en-us/library/ms188708(v=sql.90).aspx
```

1. Confirm that we can transfer files between two data centers (perhaps secure share that only the databases in question can read/write from).

2. Back up databases on USAUSDBCI2\PRDDB01.

3. Back up database(s) on USAUS11DB51\PRDRPT01.

4. Copy back up files from AUS->BOS.

5. Restore database backups from USAUSDBCI2\PRDDB01 with NORECOVERY.

6. Restore database backup(s) from USAUS11DB15\ PRDRPT01 with NORECOVERY.

7. (Step 6 handles step 1 of `http://msdn.microsoft.com/en-us/library/ms188708(v=sql.90).aspx`).

8. Confirm log-shipping is working.

9. Put up a "down for maintenance" message on the AUS web farm.

10. Consult `http://msdn.microsoft.com/en-us/library/ms191233(v=sql.90).aspx`.

11. Consult `http://msdn.microsoft.com/en-us/library/ms178117(v=sql.90).aspx`.

12. Change prodtest.disastercorp.com to point to the Franklin data center (1 minute).

13. Build replication to USBOSDB19\DRRPT01 (1 hour).

    a. May need to remove replication to USAUS11DB51\PRDRPT01.

    b. Build scripts for this!

14. Use bostest.disastercorp.com to confirm that the web farm can reach the database. (1 minute)

15. Use prodtest.disastercorp.com to confirm that the failover has worked and the data is accessible. (30 minutes)

16. Move log shipping back to AUS (details to follow).

17. Change prodtest.disastercorp.com to point to AUS data center. (1 minute)

18. Build replication to USAUS11DB51\PRDRPT01. (1 hour)

19. May need to remove replication to USBOSDB19\DRRPT01

    a. Build scripts for this!

    b. Use AUStest.disastercorp.com to confirm that the web farm can reach the database. (1 minute)

20. Remove the "down for maintenance" message.

Follow-up

Take the preceding steps and any documentation made during the test (especially the timing) and put into Disastercorp acceptable documentation.

Schedule

Target "as early as possible."

Risks

SAN replication could fail. This could result in the corruption at either or both ends. To mitigate this, backups should be maintained and a smaller dataset should be used for this test. However, it would be very useful to test with the *full* dataset, if possible.

Rollback Procedure

Risk Analysis

_____

Approval:

IT/Dev Approval: _____ Date: _____

QA Approval: _____ Date: _____

Index

A, B

Air traffic control (ATC), 37
Apollo program, 125
Application programming interface (API), 61
Automatic external defibrillator (AED), 3

C

Change/review plan (CRP), 129
    goal, 129
    log shipping, 133
    preliminary plan, 130
    reason, 130
    review, 131
    risk analysis, 135
    rollback procedure, 135
    SAN sync, 131
    schedule, 135

Change review plans (CRPs), 52, 55

Checklists
    acronyms, 48
    after-action steps, 47
    analysis, 56–57
    commercial air travel, 49–50, 54
    critical-care specialist, 46
    empty database copy, 55–56
    fact- and evidence-based, 46
    ground control, 50–51
    matrix/evaluate overall risk, 53
    overview, 45
    planning of, 51–52
    pre-printed and formalized checklist, 54
    steps of, 46, 47
    table-topping, 53–54
    types of, 46

Crew resource management (CRM), 3, 35
    air traffic control, 37
    analysis, 36
    approach, 36
    aspects, 39
    eastern airlines flight 401 vs. US airways flight 1549, 35
    Flight 232, 38
    Hayes, Captain, 40
    IT, 41–43
    Miracle, 37
    NTSB, 37
    problem descriptions, 40
    United Airlines Flight 37, 173

D, E, F, G

Disaster response (DR) plan, 85, 95
    actual testing, 4
    analysis, 6–7, 92–93, 105–106
    approach, 3, 100
    backup, 100
    business continuity plan, 88
    business operations, 85, 86
    cave-rescue, 5
    change-overs, 98
    constitutional line, 97
    corporate terms, 97
    CRM, 3
    decision making, 98
    definition, 2

Get the eBook for only $4.99!

Why limit yourself?

Now you can take the weightless companion with you wherever you go and access your content on your PC, phone, tablet, or reader.

Since you've purchased this print book, we are happy to offer you the eBook for just $4.99.

Convenient and fully searchable, the PDF version enables you to easily find and copy code—or perform examples by quickly toggling between instructions and applications.

To learn more, go to http://www.apress.com/us/shop/companion or contact support@apress.com.

Printed in the United States
By Bookmasters